THE POSTULATES

OF THE THEMATIC

Etsko Schuitema

INTENT PUBLISHING

Title: THE POSTULATES of the thematic

ISBN:978-0-620-97844-6

Published and distributed by: Intent Publishing
Schuitema Associates cc trading as Intent Publishing
Postal address: PO Box 877, Walkerville, 1876
Physical Address: 64 Cross Road, Walkers Fruit Farms, De Deur, 188

Tel: +27 11 8670587
e-mail: info@schuitemagroup.com
Website: www.schuitemagroup.com

About our logo: The square in the middle represents The One, from The One come the two surrounding lines, the 'Outward' and the 'Inward'.

Contents

FOREWORD

For those readers not familiar with Etsko's two principal works, 'Leadership – The Care and Growth Model' and 'Intent – Exploring the Core of Being Human', the origins of his thematic lay in research he conducted in the gold mining industry in the early 1980's. The issue researched was the cause of escalating conflict between management and labour on the mines, and it was found that it was attributable to deteriorating trust between the two groups. Most interestingly, it was found that the break-down in trust was not attributable to the physical conditions, perse, on the mines, but to the underlying intent of management either to exploit the labour, or to care for them and empower them. That begged the questions not only what leadership style would be most conducive to high levels of willingness amongst the workers to give of their best, but also to careful consideration of the underlying intent of the leaders themselves, in relation to the conduct of their own lives.

The result was thought-provoking analyses of what constitutes excellence in an individual, a leader and a team, and correspondingly what undermines that excellence. Over the next 25 years Etsko has written up the thematic in the two books mentioned previously and, together with his associates, has applied the model, with great success, in all types and sizes of businesses, government bodies and NGOs. More recently, he distilled the fundamental truths which underpin the thematic into a set of 68 'postulates'. These were initially set out in the final chapter of his book 'Intent'. Personally I have been unable to fault them as essential truths, and I have seen different groups which have been invited to find fault with them come to the same conclusion. Those postulates are, in themselves, very profound and thought-provoking observations on the nature of man, of the universe, of man's relation to the universe and other men, and on all social organisations.

In this book, Etsko has started with the postulates, and then written a commentary on them and on their implications. They are deeply challenging and potentially life changing for all who read them carefully, think them through, and take ownership of those which really have resonance in their own life experience. As Etsko has indicated in his introduction, the scope of the analysis is vast, ranging all the way from the maturing process, which is essential for every individual on the journey from cradle to grave, through the implications of this for families, social organisations, businesses and ultimately to governments, nations and economies.

Etsko's earlier works had already brought about fundamental shifts in my own life, even to the point of carefully assessing my intention lying behind every interaction with my fellow human beings, including my wife of 42 years. The resultant improvement in my appreciation of and gratitude to them for the roles they had played was remarkable. But this work on the postulates has considerably strengthened the foundation of my understanding of the incredibly benevolent nature of the universe; my oneness with that universe; my apparent, but false, separation from it, and consequential struggle to find a satisfactory compromise with it; and the extraordinary grace and peace which result from working consciously and persistently at returning to that condition of 'oneness', and totally subjugating the ego in the course of doing so.

I sincerely recommend this book to all conscientious seekers of truth, and those who are involved in the pursuit of excellence in the conduct of their own lives. I am in awe of it!

Bob Tucker
Former CEO of 'The Banking Council', South Africa

Introduction

I have often felt that one of the key factors that entrench the alienation of people in this age is the way in which the intelligentsia set up the study of humanness. What I mean by this is that the disciplines concerned with understanding the human being present themselves essentially in two classes, namely the psychological and the sociological. It is as if one's inner reality and the world of transaction out there are seen to be distinct and mutually exclusive areas of concern.

This bifurcation is fundamentally disabling. One's inner health is intimately connected with one acting on the basis of what is transactionally correct. This transactionally correct action is the basic building block of a just and sane society. The converse is also true. If one acts in a malevolent way, this transaction not only damages society, it also entrenches one's inner malaise, dissatisfaction and existential disquiet. The outer and inner are inseparable.

I've been increasingly convinced that the way in which the Humanities and the Social Sciences have been cut-up has created a condition where we neglect the core issues when we look at the issues of being human.

It is almost as if the phenomenon of being human has been dismembered to the point where we can no longer see the wood for the trees. In a sense the Humanities have been looking for a unified field of theory for quite some time now, and what I am proposing here is that the delivery of that unification lies at the door of the issue of intent.

'The Postulates' seeks to demonstrate that, with an articulacy regarding the issue of intent, we can construct an absolutely sensible and feasible theoretical framework in any of the human sciences, from psychology all the way through to political science. The fundamental methodology is to work from the level of the singular, of the individual, through to the collective, weaving the issue of intent throughout as the common theme.

One of the implications of this view- is that we cannot have a healthy society based on unsound individuals; and that the building blocks of groups are individuals. The logical deployment of the argument, therefore, starts off with understanding the individual; then understanding the individual in small groups like families, intimate groups, business teams; and then from there, as a continuum, understanding of the human phenomenon on the basis of macro issues like the economic and political.

Starting at the level of the individual, the key understanding that we are proposing here is that every human being on this planet is on the same trajectory, irrespective of gender, age, belief etc. We are all walking the same path, which is essentially the cradle to the grave.

'The Postulates' are the logical outcome of understanding that when we are born we are here to get unconditionally, and when we die, we give everything unconditionally. If these two fundamental assumptions are true, then all of 'The Postulates' are a logical build upon that insight. They start off with the most immediate and personal issues. 'What is my engagement with life about?'; 'What is my engagement with time about?'; 'What is my engagement with the other about?'; etc. Having explored the issue of intent with regard to the individual, 'The Postulates' buildbeings,s to an increasingly higher order of abstraction. We are, therefore, not just dealing solely with individuals, but dealing with things relating to the transaction and interaction between people, giving us a perspective on the phenomenon of being human generally. As human beings, we do not exist as individuals, we exist as social beings, and the same set of patterns of individual intent are operative at a societal level.

'The Postulates' seek to provide an alternative to the current worldview, which is fundamentally based on self-interest. This worldview is based on a set of assumptions which say that we only exist because we exist as individuals and that there is no greater continuity that subsumes the self and the other, which means that the self exists contra-distinct and opposite to the world.

This view creates a deeply competitive set of assumptions about life. The effect on the individual is that it picks up the assumptions of a being under threat.

My attempt to compete against the other is a deeply fraught prospect, in so far as the social other is numerous (there are 6-7 billion of them) and the Totality of the Other is vast beyond comprehension. This produces an undertone of fear in the register of the individual's internal dialogue, which can only have dysfunctional consequences.

The impact of this competitive mindset is also dysfunctional for groups. The consulting experience of my colleagues and I suggests that groups populated by competitive individuals have a deeply fractious character, and are only sustained with superimposed control. On the other hand, when groups are populated by co-operative individuals, they become robust. This cooperativeness of the individual is only possible because the individual sees the interests of the other and that of the self as continuous and consistent, rather than discontinuous and inconsistent.

In 'The Postulates' I seek to articulate the implications of a view that there is a super-ordinate continuity which subsumes all things, including ourselves. This means that we do not exist opposite to the world, we exist as part of the world.

To use a metaphor, your hand doesn't exist in opposition to your body; it exists as part of your body. When your hand becomes the opposite to your body we call this amputation and you no longer have a whole body or a healthy hand.

Finally, I would like to add a note on context. The observations explored in this text are the result of two parallel endeavours in my own life: my professional endeavour as a consultant and my spiritual practice as an aspirant in an inner tradition.

My professional endeavour is based on research that I conducted in the 1980's under the auspices of the 'Chamber of Mines of South Africa Research Organisation'. That work was specifically focused on understanding conflict in large organisations and provided the material for the development of a leadership model referred to as the 'Care and Growth Model'. Based on this research a group of colleagues founded a consultancy in 1990 and, over the last two decades, we have had the opportunity to refine our insights by applying them to very diverse organisations throughout the world.

It is not possible, however to sanitize this work from its origins, so there are still many, specifically South African observations in the text.

My spiritual practice has largely informed my understanding of the relationship between the issue of intent and the maturation of people. This is due to the exposure I have had to the Shadhili-Darqawi Sufi order. The order has its origins in North Africa and is informed by diverse sources, from North African Gnosticism to the mysticism of the Andalusian Arabs who were the refugees of the Reconquista.

What follows is the application of my insights from both endeavours to the world that we are in.

Chapter 1

THE TEXT

Maturation

1. It is axiomatically true that, at birth, the Totality of an infant's potential lies before it. It is, therefore, here to get in the fullest, most unconditional sense of the word. It is equally true that at the moment of death one loses it all, unconditionally. We arrive getting it all and we leave giving it all. The process of maturation which transmutes our lives implies a movement from one extreme of unconditional getting to the other of unconditional giving.

2. The difference between giving it all and having it all taken away lies in the intent of the one who is doing the giving. The process of maturation in the direction of unconditional giving is, therefore, a process of the maturation of the will, or of intention.

3. Maturity, inner wellbeing and wholesomeness are about being able to face death without regret or fear. The only useful clinical contribution to the self must therefore be about cultivating the ability and the preparedness to die at any given moment.

4. Any biographic account of the self is disabling since it focuses the attention on the past, what the self has accumulated. An enabling account of the self must, therefore, take account of the self as the self looks forward, in other words, faces death. Fundamentally this truncates the need for catharsis in the cultivation of inner health.

The Advancing and Receding Views of Time

5. One's understanding of the movement from cradle to grave can either be based on an advancing, or a receding, view of time. A receding view of time takes birth as its reference point and views life as a process of accumulation. This means that as one gets further and further away from birth one has more and more. An advancing view of time takes death as its reference point. This means that as one ages there is less and less of you. Every moment is a moment of expending potential, of handing over something. This is a view of time advancing because it is a view that is concerned with the inexorable approach of death.

6. To aspire to either wealth or knowledge is to have a receding view of time, since both of these assume that there is more and more as one gets older. To aspire to the maturation of intent is to have an advancing view of time. It is concerned with having less and less over time and being able to face the final test of disappearing with nothing at all with equanimity.

Freedom and Fulfilment

7. Intention defines interest and, therefore, attention. A person demonstrates their maturity by what they pay attention to in the world.

8. If you pay attention to what you want to get from the other, the other's ability to withhold what you want makes you manipulable. They are strong and you are weak. When you pay attention to what you should be giving to the other, the other no longer has power over you. The empowerment of the self coincides with the shift of attention of the self from taking to giving, from expectation to contribution.

9. The degree to which a person's motive is conditioned by their expectation is the degree to which they are defined by the outcome of events. The more unconditional a person is with regard to what they are contributing, the more they will define the outcome of events.

10. To construct one's intention on expectation is to become the slave and the victim of the other. Freedom is therefore concerned with basing one's intention and attention on your contribution.

11. The Totality of the Other rarely delivers a set of circumstances that coincide totally with what will satisfy the self at that time. For a person to

focus their attention on what they want from the other, therefore, cultivates discontent.

12. One's own behaviour, in other words, what one is doing to or giving to the other, is always within one's own control. To concern yourself with the nature of your contribution is, therefore, to cultivate a habit of fulfilment.

Generosity and Courage

13. A person who is here to get will focus their attention on maximizing accumulation and minimizing loss. The predominant register of their internal dialogue will be greed and fear. A person who is here to give will be concerned with cultivating the capacity to hand over both things associated with the self, and the self, itself. The predominant register of their internal dialogue will, therefore, be concerned with generosity and courage.

14. The mature self-transacting in the world will give things easily and will not be risk averse.

Benevolence and Malevolence

15. The demeanour of the immature self is fundamentally hostile and malevolent with regard to the Totality of the Other. The other is seen to be there to serve the self. The other is seen to be that which has to be changed, dismembered and demeaned to satisfy the requirements of the self. It is, therefore, accurate to identify the intention of the immature self as malevolent intention.

16. The world encapsulating the malevolent self will be in a process of extinction. It will be in chaos, decay and disorder in the process of satisfying the futile attempt of this self to establish permanence.

17. Every attempt of the malevolent self to establish order, in view of securing the self, will further entrench the process of decay and extinction of the world, which the self experiences. This extinction of the world is exponential.

18. People who are here to give are able to suspend their own comfort, convenience and interest in order to serve the other. The self accepts constraint in serving the other. The self is, therefore, expended in the care

of the other. The self is submitted to extinction and the other is cultivated. The world encapsulating this self will present itself as orderly, wholesome and well tended. Both the intention and the effect of this self will be benevolent.

19. There can be no benevolent intention without the affirmation of a greater and absolute continuity that subsumes the self and the other. The loss of conditionality implied by acting with benevolent intention is, therefore, simultaneously the process whereby the self is sublimated into this higher order continuity. The extinction of the self in the process of serving the other establishes a higher order subject that subsumes both self and other. This higher order subject is not in the world. The world is in it.

20. The more malevolent a person is, the more they will experience the other, and the good auspices of the other, to be discontinuous with the self. The malevolent self is fundamentally in a win/lose competition with the Totality of the Other.

21. The Totality of the Other presents itself as vast, majestic and unassailable next to the apparent smallness and insignificance of the self. The attempt of the malevolent self to bend the world to its will is therefore fundamentally futile. When the gnat irritates the giant long enough it gets swatted into oblivion.

22. We either give in to the process of submitting the self with good grace or we are crushed into submission by the Totality of the Other. Either way the self is destined for extinction.

Growth

23. Because a process separates birth from death, it indicates that growth or the transmutation of intent happens incrementally. Each incremental step of change has the same basic structure. The self presents the other with behaviour based on malevolent or conditional motive. In the fullness of time the other confronts this behaviour and the self is presented with failure. This failure necessitates a review of motive by the self.

24. The nature of the resistance, which the self experiences from the other, is appropriate to the level of maturity of the self. In its most infantile state the self is here to get unconditionally. The other resists this brazen lack of consideration and the self realises that it has to appease the other in order to get what it wants. It therefore 'gives in order to get.'

25. 'Giving in order to get' is about manipulating the other in order to achieve an end that the self would construe as beneficial to the self. The other disables every transaction based on this intent. Every time a transaction of this nature is disabled, the self attempts a more sophisticated strategy in order to gain control over the other. The increase in sophistication of these strategies amounts to an increased preparedness of the self to delay gratification.

26. Growth is therefore about a sublimation of intent.

27. In the process of growth, the child is introduced to the social order when it discovers that it is discontinuous from the other. This discovery is simultaneously the first apprehension of the capacity of the other to withhold the good auspices of the self, and the birth of the intent to bend the other to suit the design of the self. The core of this intent is about the managing of predictable outcomes beneficial to the self.

28. As the self matures, there is a growing insight that vanquishing the other destroys the source of the contentment of the self. There is an understanding that the self cannot achieve peace with the social other in the absence of a negotiated settlement with the social other.

The Social Order

29. The production of surpluses is an economic metaphor for a successful social order. A surplus suggests that the members of that society have produced more than they have taken out. Collectively, they have given more than they have taken.

30. The degree to which members of a society are negotiating on behalf of their own interests is the degree to which the society has cancer and is doomed to failure. This is because the intent of the individuals is to succeed at the haggle, in other words, to get as much as they can for giving as little as possible.

31. A social order may be described as a pattern of transactions between people. If the intent of the average transaction in a society is malevolent, then the society will be fractured, at war with itself and in a state of decay. The degree to which the individual engages each transaction in view of what is correct and benevolent is the degree to which the society is robust and in harmony.

32. The pursuit of transactional correctness is simultaneously the path of unfoldment of the individual and the establishment of a legitimate social order. The individual's highest self-interest therefore lies in acting consistently in the best interests of the other.

33. A society based on the pursuit of self-interest will cultivate hostility between the generations, the sexes and between the leaders and the followers.

34. A person in pursuit of his or her self-interest is fundamentally untrustworthy.

35. The degree to which there is an element of unconditional service in the intent of the self is the degree to which the self makes peace with the social order. The attempt to be of service to the other, amounts to the intent to manage outcomes beneficial to the other. While this intent is benevolent, the behaviour that flows from it is still conditional. It is benevolent 'getting to give.'

Beyond the Social Good

36. Preparedness for death implies the capacity to give unconditionally. This implies a fundamental disavowal of any pretence of usefulness or capacity to manage outcomes. 'Giving to give' implies a disregard for outcome, or what is going to be achieved. At this point, the maturation of the self requires a fundamental alienation from the social order, since death is an alienation from the social order.

37. The final fulfilment of the destiny of the individual is, therefore, beyond the social good. In this sense, the successful life is super- ordinate to the social good. The individual is super-ordinate to society. The social order is fundamentally there to enable the individual, not the other way round.

38. Societies that are concerned with the enablement of the individual are fundamentally benevolent. Societies that subordinate the enablement of the individual to the social project are fundamentally malevolent.

Moses and Pharaoh

39. In Semitic mythology this distinction is explored in the account of Moses and Pharaoh. The Pharaonic model subjugates the people to the work of the social project. This project amounts to the construction of the pyramidal mausoleum of the leader. The aim of this mausoleum is to ensure the immortality and eternal aggrandizement of the leader. The people are enslaved to this project, principally, because of their own need for the security of life in Egypt. In the Mosaic model the social project is fundamentally bizarre. It amounts to an aimless wandering through the desert for forty years. This wandering, however, is about enabling a generation of free people. The social project is, therefore, the means to the end of enabling the people, not the other way round. Moses, the leader, never gets to the Promised Land. He is expended in the process of freeing the people from slavery.

40. A Pharaonic society, therefore, subordinates the growth of the individual to the social project and the social project is about the immortality and aggrandizement of those in control. A Mosaic, or prophetic, society applies the social project to the end of enabling free and mature people, and the leadership of this society expend themselves to this end.

41. Correct leadership, therefore, entails understanding that the role of the leader is to serve or care for the followers. This care, however, is fundamentally about the growth of the individual, in other words, cultivating the individual's freedom, maturity and power. It is about cultivating the individual's capacity for unconditional benevolent action. Legitimate leadership is about the care and growth of the follower. Likewise, a legitimate social order is about the care and growth of the individual.

Governance

42. Legitimate governance is concerned with enabling the best in the citizen. This means that, at the end of a legitimate political establishment, the average citizen will be functioning at a higher level on the continuum of intent than was the case when that establishment came to power. Conversely, illegitimate governance will finish with the citizen functioning

at a lower level along the continuum of the maturation of intent than was the case when it started.

43. Illegitimate governments leave the people more greedy, selfish and needy than they found them. Conversely, legitimate governments will leave the people more courageous, honourable and generous than they found them.

44. A malevolent social order has a vested interest in the disablement of the individual. It will seek to cultivate neediness, insecurity and conditional behaviour in the individual. It is precisely this behaviour which lays the foundation for its demise.

45. The liberal defence of human rights confuses the right of the individual to be enabled with self-interest. It therefore forms part of the ideological justification of a fundamentally malevolent social order.

46. Making the social project subordinate to the individual does not imply endorsing rampant individualism and self-interest. The generation that fled Egypt found the wandering through the desert fundamentally onerous. Their own freedom meant giving up the collusion of mediocrity that gave them security. In this sense, freedom from tyranny is simultaneously freedom from Pharaonic oppression, and a disavowal of the expectation of security.

47. An enabling social order requires the individual to pursue goals that are greater than self-interest. They are goals that are fundamentally generous in character. Every incremental step of growth implies an incremental shift of intention in the direction of benevolence. This is only possible if the social other holds the individual accountable for the malevolence of their intention.

Accountability of the Citizen

48. A social order that does not hold the individual accountable for the malevolence of their intention is fundamentally disabling. Such a society can only cultivate weak, grasping, cowardly and selfish individuals. Such people will be ill equipped to face the must fundamental existential problem, namely the proximity of death.

49. It is unjust to hold a person accountable if they do not have the means or are not able to make the contribution required of them. A person

does not have the ability to contribute if they do not know why or how to make the contribution required of them.

50. For a person to know why they should do something means for them to understand the benevolent intent of the particular task or activity. It is not possible for a person to act unconditionally in the pursuit of a task that is fundamentally about taking.

51. It is not just to treat the person who behaves deliberately malevolently, and the person who does so through carelessness, in the same way. A person who behaves malevolently through carelessness should be censured. A person who behaves with deliberate malevolence should be punished. There is a difference between culpable homicide and murder.

52. The register of correction in the liberal language of justice suggests that inability, carelessness and malevolence are somehow the same thing. This assumption is both false and disastrous. It is unjust to punish a person who is unaware that he is transgressing. It is appropriate to censure a person who transgresses through carelessness. It is appropriate to punish a person who transgresses deliberately. Not to view the person who is malevolent as worthy of punishment is to sanction malevolence in the society.

53. If technocratic society requires the brazen pursuit of selfinterest to function, it also suggests that it will harbour a relatively large number of criminally disposed citizens. In fact, a degree of criminality in the population makes a functional contribution to the overall maintenance of the status quo. It cultivates the climate of insecurity, which legitimises the security apparatus of the state.

54. The assumption that imprisonment rehabilitates the criminal is both false and arrogant. Prisons foster and cultivate a culture of criminality, they do not remedy it. To imprison the criminal means to punish the victim of the crime twice: firstly, by having been the target of the crime and secondly, by being taxed to keep the criminal in prison. To hold the criminal appropriately accountable for his malevolence means to execute those guilty of violent crimes. Further, it follows that flogging and amputation for less serious crimes would be more just than imprisonment.

Rights

55. The liberal understanding of human rights fundamentally undermines the individual's accountability and, therefore, entrenches his disablement. This establishes the conditions where people are permitted to pursue and remain equal to the worst in themselves. This destroys the individual and the social order at the same time.

56. The perpetuation of the current order requires the licentiousness of the individual. It, therefore, follows that the suppression of fundamentally destructive phenomena such as promiscuity, pornography, gambling and prostitution will be construed to be contrary to basic human rights.

57. A disabled parent will not be trusted to spank her child. A disabled teacher will not be permitted to exercise corporal punishment on the pupil. A disabled employer will not be permitted to dismiss an employee. A disabled citizen will not be allowed to defend himself when attacked by a criminal. All of this suggests that the individual is not allowed to hold someone else accountable for their actions. The individual is not accountable, nor can they call someone else to account without the intercession of a super-ordinate control function. The system rules. It is super-ordinate to the individual.

Organisations

58. A company is a virtual village. The requirements for the legitimacy of the social order are, therefore, equally applicable to the company. A company that has the enrichment of the shareholder as its primary goal is basically concerned with the aggrandizement of those in control. It is therefore malevolent and disabling.

59. The view that sees organisational structure and system as super-ordinate to the individual is fundamentally Pharaonic. The bureaucratic concern with control both assumes and entrenches the untrustworthiness of the employee at work and the citizen in society. Far from empowering the individual the technocratic order diminishes him at every turn.

Control

60. The more a society is concerned with control, the more it cultivates criminality. The more sophisticated the control mechanisms are, the more ingenious the rogues become.

61. Each time a control is introduced, one shifts accountability for the thing that is being controlled from the person who is doing it to the person who is controlling it. The effect of this is that the more control you impose, the less control you have.

Economy

62. Just as it is illegitimate to ascribe significance to the social order over the individual, it is inadmissible to see the economy as super- ordinate to the transaction. A successful economic order is not one that is well managed by economic technocrats, but one in which each transaction is value adding.

63. The language of economics ascribes a scientific validity to a principally speculative exercise. Economic jargon replaces the concern with what accounts for a just transaction with a concern with what kind of system works. It is about what is pragmatic rather than what is right. It trades correctness for expediency.

64. A legitimate transaction will reflect the intention of the seller to give good measure and the intention of the buyer to reward service appropriately. The concern for both of these parties is, therefore, what is fair and just for the other, rather than getting as much as possible for giving as little as possible.

65. Any transaction in which someone gets something for nothing is fundamentally usurious and unjust.

66. The degree to which the individual transactions in the market are unjust is the degree to which the market will require super-ordinate control.

67. When the average adult makes doing the right thing their central concern there is little need for overall management of the system. There is a spontaneous order that arises in every sphere of life, from the market to the school. Such a society, basically, works. When the average adult makes getting as much as possible for as little as possible their central concern the

social order requires to be managed. Without continuous, super-ordinate control such a society collapses.

68. The modern economy is a hybrid of two tyrannies: an uncontrolled market and illegitimate transaction. This has enabled piracy on a scale unknown in human history.

Chapter 2

THE COMMENTARY

Maturation

If one views maturation as a process, then what is true for any process is that it is an incremental progression between a beginning and an end.

1. It is axiomatically true that, at birth, the Totality of an infant's potential lies before it. It is, therefore, here to get in the fullest, most unconditional sense of the word...

The very first moment that a child is alive, whatever it is going to get, it will still get. It has had nothing yet. It has only had its first breath. This means that all that it is still to receive in its life, will come. In this sense the child is here to get in the most unconditional sense of the word, insofar as it is true for that child.

It is equally true that at the moment of death one loses it all unconditionally. We arrive getting it all and we leave giving it all. The process of maturation which transmutes our lives implies a movement from one extreme of unconditional getting to the other of unconditional giving.

An appropriate challenge to this would be 'Listen! When I die I don't give anything, but everything gets taken away from me'. This is probably the most obvious reaction, but implies a further question 'What is the difference between giving something and having something taken away from you?' The answer lies with the issue of intent.

When I give you something, I intend to give it. When it is taken from me, I lose it, even though I didn't intend to give it. For example, a person who has a thousand dollars stolen from them is very different to the person who gave somebody a thousand dollars. But that difference doesn't sit in the object of the dollars. It sits in the subject of the person who is going through the experience. More specifically, it sits in the intention of the person who is going through the experience.

A further question could be asked: whether death is painful to the person who is willing to give everything. The key to understanding this has to do with resistance. For example, if while I was preparing to cook something for lunch I cut my finger with a knife, the physical stimulus of the pain presents me with two possibilities. I can, at that point, resist what was happening; in other words, frame it as an incredible imposition on my life. From one point of view, it is, as I would have to go and bandage my finger to prevent myself bleeding all over the food, and it is of course, very painful. I could therefore tell myself it is a great imposition, that it is awful, a great pity and something to be regretted. But in my experience, I have found that when I do this, I actually experience the pain more acutely.

There is another way of dealing with the pain, which is to let it wash over you. If you do not resist it, you experience yourself as almost transparent, so that it just passes through you. So what occurs to me at the point when I cut my finger is that I can turn this into a crisis, or I can just submit to the experience.

When you submit to the experience and acknowledge that it is just there, without judging it, it is not so bad. The same must be true at death. When you die you might experience pain, but you can choose not to resist the pain. Then the experience passes over you, through you. It is not construed as a problem.

2. The difference between giving it all and having it all taken away lies in the intent of the one who is doing the giving. The process of maturation in the direction of unconditional giving is, therefore, a process of the maturation of the will, or of intention.

One of the implications of these first two postulates is that we have to review the nature of this progression, which we refer to as maturation or growth. Intuitively we view growth as a cumulative process. Every point of progression is about getting something more, about accumulating something. It's about writing up another achievement or result into our biographic account.

The alternative way of looking at growth is not that it is about getting somewhere; it is about leaving something behind. You can only occupy a place, which is bigger and better than where you are now, if you leave where you are behind. This means that for growth to happen in the moment requires loss in the moment, because by definition, what we are growing into, is in the future.

As we get older we are busy losing something. We are giving more and more. Every moment we move forward, we are busy handing over a piece of our potential. The process of maturation is a process of incremental, ongoing, giving. If we look at it from this point of view, it gives us the opportunity to completely change our take on our psychological health.

The current take on psychological health is fundamentally biographic. If I have an ailment, if I wake-up in the morning with a post-traumatic tick in my left eye, sweaty palms and a very legitimate feeling that the universe is out to get me, and I go to a therapist, what he is likely to do is ask me to recant a very long biographical narrative: What happened when I was two, what happened when I was four, all the cruel things my mother did to me and so on.

This implies that we have to do a massive biographical revisit in order to become healthy. What we are arguing here is that our health is not about orientating backwards into the past. Health is about the degree to which you are able to unconditionally face the world as it approaches you. It is about the propensity to face death with equanimity. It is about the ability to give or lose unconditionally.

So a biographic account is only helpful insofar as it helps us to find those hooks that are keeping us from being properly orientated forward to life, as it comes towards us. This insight introduces the next two postulates.

3. Maturity, inner wellbeing and wholesomeness are about being able to face death without regret or fear. The only useful clinical contribution to the self must therefore be about cultivating the ability and the preparedness to die at any given moment.

4. Any biographic account of the self is disabling since it focuses the attention on the past, what the self has accumulated. An enabling account of the self must, therefore, take account of the self as the self looks forward, in other words, faces death. Fundamentally this truncates the need for catharsis in the cultivation of inner health.

From what I have understood, most clinical, psychological models have a very high regard for the cathartic process. This means an ongoing revisit of biography to find out what the issues are in your life. From the point of view of Sufism, the inner tradition I have some personal experience with, this is not necessary. From this point of view, psychological health is about the ability to constantly face the moment that we are in, without regret or fear, and with the intention to hand over unconditionally.

As we try to hand over unconditionally to whatever life puts in front of us, we sometimes experience hooks or snags that make it difficult to face the oncoming moment squarely and with equanimity. These hooks or snags do very often have a biographical root. When we deal with that particular piece of biography correctly, our attention is unhooked, enabling us to face the moment with full attention. This enables us to take that next incremental step. This suggests that the clarification of biography does not require an exhaustive recapitulation of biography; it requires the incremental dealing with issues as they become apparent.

In other words, you don't fix yourself, life fixes you. The process of fixing is concerned with our incremental washing off of our conditioning over time, step by step. As we know, it is the two hands that wash each other. From the point of view of the self, the other hand is the other, it is the world. It is life.

Shaykh Muhammad Ibn al-Habib, a teacher in the Sufi tradition, was once approached by a student who complained bitterly about his wife. The shaykh listened for a while and then became annoyed. 'Be quiet', he told the student. 'Why?', the student asked. 'You clearly don't know the purpose of a spouse', the shaykh replied. 'The purpose of a spouse is like water in a vessel. It is the nature of the water to find out where the cracks in the vessel are. It is poor courtesy for the vessel to complain when the water finds the cracks!'

As we live, the other, the spouse, the boss, life itself, does things to us that exposes our conditional motive. This conditional motive is invariably about what we want to get from life rather than what we are willing to give. All conditional motive is based on some kind of conditioning, some biographically based conviction about life, which is more often than not both false and inappropriate to the situation. In the first instance, escaping that conditioning is often as easy as just acting contrary to it. Sometimes, however, it is deeply entrenched and cannot just be contradicted behaviourally. At these times revisiting biography is useful.

Growth is, therefore, not about this narcissistic and morbid wallowing in the biography of the past. It is about engaging with the world as it comes toward us as honestly as we can, with the intent to do the best for the other in the situation we are in. We are like a vessel submerged in the water of the Totality of the Other. When we start springing leaks, we can use this as an opportunity to understand where the cracks in the vessel are. This then helps us to direct the appropriate attention, to the inner work required, to achieve wholesomeness.

At the root of this approach to psychological health is the conviction that our lives are not a process of accumulation, they are in fact a process of expenditure, of handing over.

The Advancing and Receding Views of Time

In order to examine how time arises for us it is necessary to first take a look at space. Most psychologists seem to agree that an infant's experience is that they are completely connected to the world that they are in. There is no sense of a distinction between self and other. That sense of distinction happens over time because the self comes to understand that the other has power over the self and can withhold the good auspices of the self. At this point the strategy of the self changes to one principally concerned with getting the other to do what the self wants it to do.

This means that simultaneous to discovering that the other is separate from the self (it is over there and self is over here), there is an insight that fulfilment is later on and need is now. That seems to start for an individual probably after the first six months of life. In other words, when you discover other is not the same as self, time is created for you. Future is created for you. Needing to get things from the future is created for you, the moment you have a sense of the self existing independently from the other.

This suggests that our experience of time happens simultaneously with our experience of existing as an individual, as a separate individual. In essence, time is a construct. If we say that it's possible to have an experience where we are completely connected with the rest of existence, where we don't experience ourselves as an individual, it also means that it must be possible to escape the tyranny of time. Time becomes irrelevant for us, because all that we ever have is the moment that we are in.

Eckhart Tolle has phrased it nicely for us. He says our sense of time requires the past and the future. The only thing that there ever is, is now. We have to 'imagine' the future and we have to 'remember' the past which means these are just electronic agitations in the brain. All that ever actually exists is the moment that confronts us, so to have something other than the moment that we are in, is to live in a construct.

Time is created as soon as we are dissatisfied with what is. Our sense of space, our sense of locality, of being distinct from other, and our sense of being in time are related things. Space and time, in terms of our experience, are related things. The degree to which I experience myself as separate from other is the degree to which I have anxiety about outcomes; I will have anxiety about the future, I have to get the other to do what I want, etc. The degree to which that happens is the degree to which I experience fulfilment to be in the future. This means I am removed from now. I introduce time into my experience.

5. One's understanding of the movement from cradle to grave can either be based on an advancing, or a receding, view of time. A receding view of time takes birth as its reference point and views life as a process of accumulation. This means that as one gets further and further away from birth one has more and more. An advancing view of time takes death as its reference point. This means that as one ages there is less and less of you. Every moment is a moment of expending potential, of handing over something. This is a view of time advancing because it is a view that is concerned with the inexorable approach of death.

6. To aspire to either wealth or knowledge is to have a receding view of time, since both of these assume that there is more and more as one gets older. To aspire to the maturation of intent is to have an advancing view of time. It is concerned with having less and less over time and being able to face the final test of disappearing with nothing at all with equanimity.

Insofar as a receding view of time bases contentment on accumulation, the fundamental patterning of intent can be construed as an emptiness that seeks to be filled. The self is experienced as something hollow, which can only be filled by other than self.

It is possible to escape this perpetual thirst. Having an advancing view of time makes the critical variable not what one has accumulated, but how eloquently and appropriately one has given. The flow of intent is not from other to self, it is from self to other. One can, therefore, describe the intent of the person, who commits fully to an advancing view of time, as a fullness that empties rather than an emptiness that seeks to be filled. For a person with an advancing view of time, fulfilment is not the motive of action; it is the foundation of action.

These two people are radically different. The person with a receding view of time is needy. This amounts to an experience of deep, existential disquiet, which manifests in an inability to be in the moment. Their effect on the world is fundamentally destructive. They deal with the other on the basis of what is good for the self.

A person with an advancing view of time is content with the moment. They have enough. They, therefore, do not need to go elsewhere to get more. Actually, they are not trying to escape the other, or the moment, at all. They are trying to take care of the other. Their effect on the other is therefore fundamentally benign.

These first six postulates, therefore, create the axiomatic basis on which the rest of the postulates are founded. They explore the basic implications of viewing maturation as a process from birth to death. The commencement of the framework is the assumption that when an infant is born it is here to get, in the most unconditional sense of the word.

It could, however, be argued that whatever an infant is going to give it will still give, and this is true. However, consider how the infant faces the moment. It is clear that in the moment that the child is born nothing is required of it. It is going to get. Nobody says to it, 'You can't pee now!', or 'It's not convenient for you to eat now.' In that sense, an infant is here to get in the fullest and most unconditional sense of the word. Nothing is required of the infant. Therefore, being here to get absolutely everything is most true at that moment.

From that point forward there is already an interplay of expectation, because the child learns that if it googles and smiles at the mother, the mother won't do cruel things to it. There is an interplay and an understanding grown through the experience of engagement and interaction with the other. When the self does something, something else comes back. There is a response. But, in our very first moment this cannot be true.

A further challenge to this view would be to ask 'What else do you have other than the moment?' This is also true. We only have the moment. The moments of birth and death differ from any other moment, however, because they do have this unconditional character. The infant in the first moment doesn't need to give anything at all. The person in their last moment has to give everything. This is hardwired into our condition.

It is, therefore, very important to remember what this means when one considers the problem of our own aspirations and what we give priority to. Anything that is concerned with accumulation is building a biographic account. Our lives, however are sealed by death. Death does not test our skill at accumulation; it tests our ability to lose unconditionally. Death tests our ability to be bigger than our biography, bigger than our accumulations, bigger than the story of what we have developed for our lives.

From this point of view, the hallmark of the maturity of a person is, how easily they can lose absolutely everything, now. Their maturity is a direct correlation of their freedom, their ability to walk away from everything without regret and without fear.

So, if the appropriate response to finding biographic stuff in the deck of our lives is to jettison it, the question arises as to whether there is any usefulness to a biographic examination at all? I think there is. The truth of the matter is that sometimes we find it very difficult to look forward with trust and equanimity. The measure of the degree to which this is the case, is the degree to which the register of our internal dialogue resonates with rancour, regret or guilt.

When this becomes apparent, the usefulness of a biographic examination is to identify experiences on which the conviction that the self, or other, is somehow untrustworthy, is based. These experiences form hooks that pull us off balance and make it difficult to view what is in front of us in a balanced way, or to do what is appropriate.

For example, I may have a significant issue of regret in my life related to my children, because when I was a young man I was very hard on them. This puts me in a position where I tolerate things I really should be confronting. Clearly, for me to deal with them appropriately now means that I have to transcend the regret of the past.

Until I transcend that regret I cannot be trusted to behave appropriately with regard to my children. Mercifully, my wife provides the necessary ballast to protect them from the inappropriate indulgence that my regret solicits.

The most profound work we can do, therefore, is to transmute the character of our regret, ill-feeling and resentment, into gratitude. These things disable our ability to act appropriately. But how do you know that you've transcended them? You start acting appropriately.

We come into this world as scintillating, pure and magical beings. Over time we learn a story, a biographic story, which we increasingly identify with. This story gets layered up in accumulated accretion, and every layer further alienates us from our original state of connectedness with all things. This process is both natural and appropriate. This accumulation is not only a concretisation of identity; it is simultaneously about the acquisition of the language and dutifulness that makes us a useful person amongst others.

In the latter half of our lives we are visited by an increasing disquiet, brought on by the proximity of death. We have an instinctive yearning to regain the paradise lost, a desire to take unadulterated pleasure in the moment as it unfolds, rather than dealing with it as another throw of the dice in a cumulative game of gain and loss. Our basic demeanour toward life seeks to move from an intent to outwit, to an intent to co-operate; from an intent to dominate, to an intent to submit.

We have two tools which enable this process: cleaning the outside and cleaning the inside. Cleaning the outside is concerned with the intent to do what is appropriate to the other in the moment, without a concern for the consequence to the self. Cleaning the inside amounts to the commitment to see all things that are presented to the self, in the moment, as fundamentally benign and, in the final analysis, in the best interest of the self. When this is not possible it may be necessary to revisit the bits of biography that militate against this view.

Freedom and Fulfilment

The foregoing postulates explore the changes in intention of people as they mature. This provides a foundation to examine the nature of the engagement of the self with the world, the other in general and other people in particular.

7. Intention defines interest and, therefore, attention. A person demonstrates their maturity by what they pay attention to in the world.

If we pay attention to what we want to get from the other, the other's ability to withhold makes us manipulable. They become strong, and we become weak. The implication of this, therefore, is that we become victims when we give attention to what we are getting from the world. Conversely, we are empowered, or freed, by giving attention to our contribution.

The difference between the way of the victim and the way of freedom has four implications. There are four attributes that are the immediate and logical implication of putting our attention on what we want from the world, and conversely, there are four attributes that are the immediate consequence of constructing our attention on what we should be giving.

These four attributes are the main reasons why people do anything at all. They are, in a sense, the core motives of people. If we ask people why they go to work, for instance, the answers that they give can be classed in four categories (not necessarily in this order):

The first reason has to do with security. For example, people will say that they go to work in order to earn a living, to put a roof over their heads and to put food on the table.

The second reason people give has to do with fulfilment. People would say things like: they love to have a sense of challenge in their job, they work to achieve a sense of job satisfaction and to have a fulfilling work life.

The third reason people go to work is about power or social status. It is about becoming significant to others, having authority and an achievement of seniority in their work life.

Finally, it often important for people to feel that they are doing something useful in the world; that they feel that their work makes a real contribution to the lives of others. One can refer to this intent as the sincere desire for harmony with the social other. These four reasons are a consequence of placing one's attention on what one is giving.

Let us start by examining the issues of security and fulfilment. When you make your security and fulfilment dependent on what you get from the world, you are making these things a dependent variable you cannot control. The universe rarely gives you what you want, when you want it. This means that when you construct your attention on what you want from the world, and if you construct your sense of fulfilment and security on the basis of what you want from the world, you will never be secure and you will never be fulfilled.

This is the nature of things. The universe cannot deliver to you your expectations at any given point in time. So if what makes you secure or fulfilled is dependent on what you are getting, you will never be secure or fulfilled. It is intriguing that people work in order for security, assuming that these things are to be found, in the job, with the other etc. They work to get some security, to get a sense of fulfilment, but they stay miserable and insecure.

Conversely, you will always have control over the quality of what you are contributing. This means that if we make the source of our security and fulfilment the quality of what we are contributing, we are more likely to become secure and fulfilled. Meaning, when we construct our work and engagement with the other on what we want to get, we stay insecure and discontented. When we construct our engagement with the other on our contribution, the more secure and fulfilled we become. And the more unconditional we are about our contribution, the more this becomes true.

This logic also has an implication for the issue of power and harmony. If I want something from you, your ability to withhold what I want gives you power over me. I am, therefore, weak. If I want to give you something, you have no power over me. In other words, my strength is based on what I'm putting in.

While I'm dealing with you on the basis of what I want from you, your ability to withhold what I want makes you dangerous to me, because you can manipulate me. And not only that, I'm dangerous to you because I want something from you. When two people are dangerous to each other, you are going to have conflict. Conversely, if I shift my attention from what I want to what I should be putting in, because you can't withhold from me anymore, and you no longer have power over me. I'm safe from you, and at the same time you are safe from me, because I am trying to be helpful to you. We then have harmony.

The core things we aspire to as human beings: security, fulfilment, a sense of power and a sense of harmony with the world around us, are to be found at the same door - the intent to give, unconditionally. The more we construct our lives on the intent to contribute, the more we harvest those four fruits.

8. If you pay attention to what you want to get from the other, the other's ability to withhold what you want makes you manipulable. They are strong and you are weak. When you pay attention to what you should be giving to the other, the other no longer has power over you. The empowerment of the self coincides with the shift of attention of the self from taking to giving, from expectation to contribution.

9. The degree to which a person's motive is conditioned by their expectation is the degree to which they are defined by the outcome of events. The more unconditional a person is with regard to what they are contributing the more they will define the outcome of events.

These two postulates progress our understanding of power a little further. The degree to which you construct your life on what leaves you, rather than what is coming towards you, is the degree to which you are not disrupted by the development of events, particularly if they don't suit you. This is why it is so important that we should examine ourselves. If my life is dependent on outcomes, outcomes define me. When things do not go my way, I experience the implications as catastrophic.

If the principle issue for us is the appropriateness of our response or contribution, we are keeping a constant eye on what we have power over. We are not knocked off balance by things that do not go our way. We patiently persevere, because getting the outcome is not the point, making the contribution is. Paradoxically, this very relentlessness is what gives people who contribute, power over outcomes.

A practical use of the above in cultivating mastery is to allow for reflection at the end of the day. The questions to ask are 'What compromised me today? Where did I get impatient? Where did I get irritated? Where did I get annoyed? Where did I experience that I did not get what I wanted?'

The issue is not to spend a sleepless night working out more intelligent strategies to get what you want. What the frustration helps to surface for you is the nature of your conditional motive. When we feel thwarted, it is because we are trying to control outcomes.

It is equally important to remember that the feeling of being thwarted is not only an issue of being confronted with outcomes that are in your immediate self-interest. One can also feel thwarted in conditions that could be considered benign. I may have an expectation, for example, that my son shouldn't smoke. I catch him smoking and have this deep sense of disappointment. Clearly, my expectation of my son is thwarted.

Now, I am not suggesting I should not challenge my son, but the degree to which this creates emotional baggage for me - 'Oh you disappointed me, and I'm such a failure as a parent etc.' - indicates that I am still trying to manage an outcome. So managing outcomes isn't just managing outcomes that are in the interest of self; it is also managing outcomes that the self considers as benign or in the interest of the other.

So this is not to suggest that we should never take control. If the building is burning down, we all owe a significant debt of gratitude to the authoritarian who takes charge and frogmarches us out the building. The issue is not that we do not take control where necessary; the issue is that we have a whimsical and dispassionate investment in the outcome. To take the frog-march metaphor further, we are more interested in the marching, than the outside of the building!

What we are trying to clarify here is how the issue of intent operates. The degree to which our intent is conditional, is the degree to which we will have a sense of frustration when things don't go the way we wanted, or expected them to go, even if we wanted them to go in a benign way. The point is not that you shouldn't intervene and do things, the issue is to forego a vested interest in the outcome.

To further illustrate this, let us say that you and I undertake a road trip and we decide we're going to take our time so that we can enjoy the journey. It so happens that trying to get to our destination proves to be practically impossible, as we breakdown in a city in the middle of nowhere. At that point we have a choice as to whether we are going to get completely frustrated and freak out because we didn't get to our destination, or we decide that we are going to have a great time in the city we broke down in.

This has got nothing to do with the breakdown. This has everything to do with how we choose to make the best of the ball life has tossed at us. We may discover it's a perfectly nice place we ended up in. We will discover things that we would have just driven past without noticing. The more you do not make the entire point the outcome you want, the more you discover the real treasures you normally rush past.

10. **To construct one's intention on expectation is to become the slave and the victim of the other. Freedom is therefore concerned with basing one's intention and attention on your contribution.**

11. **The Totality of the Other rarely delivers a set of circumstances that coincide totally with what will satisfy the self at that time. For a person to focus their attention on what they want from the other, therefore, cultivates discontent.**

12. **One's own behaviour, in other words, what one is doing or giving to the other, is always within one's own control. To concern yourself with the nature of your contribution is, therefore, to cultivate a habit of fulfilment.**

My son challenges me on this point. His view is that this pursuit of contentment sounds quite selfish. He thinks that the world needs changing; that it is in such a sad state, that it requires people who care enough about outcomes to intervene in its best interest, and this of course is true. But I remain convinced that the most dramatic thing you can do in this world, is to change your own intent.

To illustrate my view, let us examine the utopian programmes of the last two centuries. The common denominator of the Fascist movements of the 1930's and 40's, the Marxist movements of the last century and the current millenarian, religious, fundamentalist movements, is that they all held as their intent, the creation of a better world.

What they share is an unconditional commitment to outcome and an expedient take on process. They will do whatever needs to be done to achieve that end, no matter how brutal. So, what I am suggesting here is that it is much more important to be unconditional about the process and open-ended about the outcome. Expressed from a sporting point of view, winning is not everything, but playing the game well and honourably is.

As this text progresses I will seek to demonstrate that outcomes do not need to be managed by us because life works, and it works spontaneously. We are not required to make the world work, but to do what is required of us in the moment that we are in. When we adopt this attitude the outcome is always benign.

Our bodies attest to a creative genius that sits behind all phenomena. That creative genius operates on the most macroscopic to the most microscopic levels of abstraction. When we allow that spontaneous sense of creative genius to operate, the outcomes are always optimal. For example, an economic market populated by people who are transacting honourably and justly, needs very little external control.

A spontaneous order manifests, in the appropriate flow of goods and services from those who have them, to those who need them.

However, we rarely look at economy from the point of view of the intent of the individual transactor. More often than not we assume that the individual is an untrustworthy pirate and spend our time finding ingenious ways to thwart his conniving, by interfering in the system within which he transacts. Intervention at the level of the system, is always against the backdrop of some utopia, some idealist outcome.

Generosity and Courage

So far, what we have been arguing is that there are fundamentally two ways of looking at life. One is that that I act consistently with the view that I'm here to get. When I do this I construct my life on the basis of an ongoing accumulation. The other is to base my intent on the conviction that I am here to give. In other words, I don't exist because I get things, I exist because I hand things over; I give.

We have argued that if fulfilment and freedom are about what we are accumulating, in the light of death, all of our endeavours are fundamentally futile. In the fullness of time all achievements or accumulations are made naught. However, if you look at fulfilment and freedom as the ability to give unconditionally, death does not solicit an argument or any resistance. If our habit is to give, we do not experience the requirement to give as a negation, we experience it as an affirmation. We are at one with what is happening to us.

13. A person who is here to get will focus their attention on maximizing accumulation and minimizing loss. The predominant register of their internal dialogue will be greed and fear. A person who is here to give will be concerned with cultivating the capacity to hand over both things associated with the self, and the self, itself. The predominant register of their internal dialogue will, therefore, be concerned with generosity and courage.

14. The mature self transacting in the world will give things easily and will not be risk averse.

Being here to give is not necessarily about being nice. Being here to give is about being appropriate and appropriate is often not nice. We can use two examples to illustrate this. If a hungry child asks John for food, the appropriate thing for John to do is to give the child food. We call this quality generosity, because it's about the giving of things On the other hand, if a strapping young lad called Dave is walking through a park and comes across a little old lady being beaten up by a thug, the appropriate thing for him to do would be to confront

the thug and give him a good hiding. We refer to the quality that Dave requires to enable him to do this as courage.

If we look at these two examples behaviourally, we are confronted by an apparent contradiction. The result of John's 'giving' was a full stomach. The result of Dave's 'giving' was a thick ear. John's giving involved sweetness and indulgence. Dave's giving involved confrontation and violence. Clearly, giving is not always about being nice, it is about being appropriate.

Every moment that confronts us has a sense of what is appropriate, what the moment requires from us. Giving means we act consistently with this sense of what is appropriate. The sense of what is appropriate is presented to us in two broad classes. There is the giving of things associated with the self, which we call generosity. Then there is the giving of the self itself, which we call courage. Courage generally asks a higher price than generosity, because generosity puts things at risk, whereas courage puts the self at risk.

If giving is about being appropriate, it is about paying the correct price that the situation dictates. Taking, then, has to mean getting the logic wrong. Like acting in a situation that requires generosity in a so- called courageous way and vice-versa. For example, should John give the hungry child a thick ear for having the cheek to ask for food, we would not consider this an attribute of John's courage, we would see it as selfishness. On the other hand, should Dave take the bag from the old lady and give it to the thug we would not see this as an attribute of his generosity, but rather an act of cowardice.

If you are in a situation that requires generosity and you act in a so-called courageous way, you are not giving, you are taking. We call that selfishness. If you are in a situation that requires courage and you act in a so-called generous way, you are not giving, you are taking. We call that cowardice.

The register of the internal dialogue of a person, who is fundamentally here to take, is to maximise gain and minimise loss. Their relationship with things will emphasise accumulation rather than giving, a quality which we experience as greed or selfishness. This necessarily means that their experience of the possibility of loss (which we have posited to be inevitable) is a cause for anxiety or fear.

The register of their internal dialogue, therefore, will be greed and fear.

We may ask what sits behind this? Why is it that I want to get more things? Why is it that greed is an issue in my life? Why should I need to accumulate? This is predicated on a view that I haven't yet received enough. The internal dialogue of a selfish person has a register of resentment, which typifies how they are thinking of themselves in the situation they are in.

A person who is here to contribute is not trying to get more from life. When they look at the moment they have no accusation. They do not say, 'I haven't had enough yet, I need to get more.' They are saying that there is more than enough, 'I have more than enough so therefore I can give freely.' So, what enables a transformation of our internal register of greed, to an internal register of generosity? It is a deliberate shift from resentment, to gratitude. A grateful person has something to give. A resentful person wants to get something.

If we examine the relationship between courage and cowardice it becomes apparent that a person who is cowardly cannot take the risk to do what is right and appropriate in the situation that they are in. It means they apprehend the future with a sense of distrust. They are saying the world is a dangerous place and if they don't look after themselves they will be vulnerable and at risk, they will be taken out. They can't afford to put themselves on the line or take a risk. The attitude that sits behind an internal dialogue of fear is distrust.

A courageous person can trust life because they are convinced that life has a design, which is bigger than their own ingenuity. They know they don't have to cover their own back all the time. They have concluded that, since they are still alive, is necessarily looking after them.

When they contrast the vastness of the universe that confronts them with their own puny nature, the number of things that could, at any point in time, go wrong with disastrous consequences for them personally; they will conclude that statistically the odds of annihilation beat the odds of continuity moment by moment. So why are they still there? This can only mean that the Totality of the Other is not arbitrary and admits a sense of design. Further to that, this sense of design is deliberately benevolently disposed to the self. This person can trust because they inhabit a friendly, rather than a hostile, universe. The person who is here to take looks at the past with resentment and looks forward at the future with distrust. The nature of these two attributes is that resentment is primary and distrust, secondary. If I examine my past and conclude that life has done me more ill than good, I will not trust life as it unfolds into the future. On the other hand, the degree to which I conclude that life has done me more good than ill, is the degree to which I will trust life as it unfolds.

This suggests that the key flaw that disables our pursuit of the fulfilment which we aspire to is resentment, and the key virtue that enables it is gratitude. Transforming the register of our internal dialogue, from resentment to gratitude, lies at the heart of our endeavour to cultivate contentment.

This deliberate cultivation of gratitude also lays the foundation for the capacity to trust, which is what enables one to take risks. If we want to find the genesis of risk aversion, we must first look for resentment. If we want to cultivate the courage that enables the appetite for risk, then we should cultivate gratitude.

The current predominant worldview is one based on self interest. It is predicated on an individual who looks at life from a vantage point of resentment. This resentment is not only deeply dysfunctional to the self, it produces a dysfunctional engagement between the self and the other. As we have observed previously, if I think you owe me, my natural inclination is to go and get from you what I think you owe me. Because that is my fundamental intent with regard to you, you will experience me as dangerous to you. Also your ability to withhold what I want, makes you dangerous to me. We are dangerous to each other and in a state of conflict.

In other words, far from being a virtue, resentment and discontentment are deeply harmful to those surrounding the person who has it, as well as to the person who has it. The nature of all conditional motive is that it produces discontentment in the person who has it. If I'm doing something to get something else, that doing is the price I have to pay in order to get what I want. If I need to pay a price in the present it is a loss that I have to endure to get something in the future. But since it is only the present that exists, that means that the experience of my life is that of loss. The degree to which I do something for conditional motive, is the degree to which my life experience is onerous and the cause of discontentment.

Benevolence and Malevolence

The worldview concerned with self-interest produces people who are in conflict with themselves and with the world. Our survival as individuals and as groups is, therefore, dependent on transmuting our resentment to gratitude. This review will help us fundamentally change our view of why we are here. It will enable the conclusion that we are not here to get anything, we are here to give.

This conviction introduces us to a new and deeply enchanting relationship with the universe that we are in. We will discover that the universe is not hostile to us, it is on our side. The interests of the self and the interest of the Totality of the Other are continuous. We are not separate from the other; we are deeply connected with it. There is a oneness that connects all things, and every time that we act in the best interest of the other we transcend, for that moment, the illusion and alienation that we exist separately from it.

The current worldview is fundamentally destructive, because it creates actions that are based on greed and fear, that are rooted in resentment and distrust. There is a far more wholesome way of looking at life, one that bases the grounds of the intent of the individual on gratitude and, therefore, solicits the will to serve.

15. The demeanour of the immature self is fundamentally hostile and malevolent with regard to the Totality of the Other. The other is seen to be there to serve the self. The other is seen to be that which has to be changed, dismembered and demeaned to satisfy the requirements of the self. It is, therefore, accurate to identify the intention of the immature self as malevolent.

There is a paradox that is operative here: When you consider yourself to exist as an individual, you are faced with the problem that the self is fundamentally, very small and the other is very big. The result of this is that the principle strategy of being alive is to try and outwit and to dominate the other. When that which is small faces that which is very big, the strategy of that which is small is to try to control or dominate that which is big. When we are vulnerable we seek to protect ourselves by controlling that which makes us vulnerable. The problem with this is that it is an unworkable prospect. It is the nature of that which is big to supersede and overcome that which is small.

This implies that the root of our assumption that we exist as individuals, is one of fundamental terror. That terror gets translated into brutality and that brutality becomes thoughtlessness. It really doesn't matter what I do to the world in order to maintain myself, because the world is very big, therefore I can consume it, I can damage it and I can break or manipulate it to satisfy my own requirements.

The key implication of the assumption that we exist as individuals is a sense of victimhood, a sense of 'I am a small thing, dominated by a big universe, and I've got to get my own out of it.' The demeanour of the self when it considers that it exists as an individual, is fundamentally hostile to the world. This hostility sets the world up as fair game. Whatever I do to the other is fundamentally acceptable. I have to make sure that my interests are protected. My demeanour then becomes malevolent and the effect on the world around me becomes destructive.

Self-interest is currently the predominant intent of the average adult citizen of the global village, which has somewhere between 6 and 7 billion inhabitants. The collective effect of this on the world must be monstrously malevolent, which is why the world we live in is in a process of extinction. To see the matter other than this is not seeing the thing as it is. In order to secure the self we destroy the world.

16. The world encapsulating the malevolent self will be in a process of extinction. It will be in chaos, decay and disorder in the process of satisfying the futile attempt of this self to establish permanence.

On one hand, when I serve, I become part of a oneness, which connects me to all things. The prospect of extinction of the self is then neither frightening nor threatening, because of my awareness that I am part of a continuity that persists. On the other hand, when I consider myself to exist as an individual, then the prospect of the loss of my individual life is horrifying. It creates the conditions where I live under the cloud of terror that is the imminence of my extinction, all the time. That terror, of imminent extinction, is the root of the malevolence of my actions.

This extinction is not just about physical death. We have to understand that the individual self faces a prospect, which is deeper, more profound, than death. It is absolute extinction. There is still a sense of benignancy in the idea of death, a sense of release. With the idea of extinction, there is just the sense of empty horror. People who exist as individuals don't die. They become extinct. They are extinguished. That which they spend their whole life fighting to stave off, the inevitable pressure coming from the Totality of the Other, eventually overwhelms them. They cease to exist, they are extinguished. They are as if they never were.

17. Every attempt of the malevolent self to establish order in view of securing the self, will further entrench the process of decay and extinction of the world, which the self experiences. This extinction of the world is exponential.

The essence of this postulate is: the more control you try to impose, the less control you have. Every strategy that the self engages to preserve itself is based on the assumption that the self can continue over time. It presupposes continuity. It presupposes that there is a tomorrow, or this afternoon, or next year etc. All strategies that are concerned with maintaining the self are control strategies. They are strategies that have, as their fundamental intent, the perpetuation of the self by producing predictable outcomes.

The universe and the other are profoundly ill-disposed to the attempt of the self to try and produce an outcome. How do we know this? We have been given a social world which acts as the theatre or schoolyard, where we can learn the rules that are operative between ourselves and the Totality of the Other.

Consider, for example, what happens between the self and other people. If you are dealing with somebody who is obviously trying to control you, your natural and intuitive reaction with regard to that person is to resist what they are trying to do to you. People hate being manipulated and having things taken from them.

When the self engages the other from the point of view of trying to secure an outcome through the other, the self creates a hostile other. The more we try to establish control, the more that which we are trying to control becomes hostile towards us and will resist what we are trying to do.

The nature of the social other is that they are numerous and we are one. It is the nature of the many to outflank the one. The nature of the Totality of the Other is that it is infinite and we are puny. It is the nature of that which is vast to annihilate that which is puny. By putting ourselves opposite to the other we are picking a fight which could not be more unevenly matched. We are going to lose.

This loss is a loss of control over the outcome, which makes us even more insecure and more in need of control. The more we try to control, the more profound is the resistance to our control, which ultimately means we have even less control. It is an horrendous, vicious circle: the more control you impose, the less control you have.

The world is set up in such a way that everything that we do which is concerned with trying to secure our own future will come back to bite us, in the fullness of time. The Totality of the Other clearly has a sense of humour. From every point of view the self is the powerless one, the beholden one; the one handed over to that which is greater. You cannot escape the Totality of the Other. Wherever you turn you are faced by the Totality of the Other. There is no hiding place and no escape! You are beholden to it, it is in charge.

18. People who are here to give are able to suspend their own comfort, convenience and interest in order to serve the other. The self accepts constraint in serving the other. The self is, therefore, expended in the care of the other. The self is submitted to extinction and the other is cultivated. The world encapsulating this self will present itself as orderly, wholesome and well tended. Both the intention and the effect of this self will be benevolent.

When I change the other in order to preserve myself, my own existence, I destroy the other and paradoxically I am also destroyed, because the other becomes hostile to me. The death of Stalin is a useful example of this. Stalin was in the habit of inviting key associates to dinner, an affair that included much drinking and continued into the wee hours of the morning. If you were one of these key people, you knew you had fallen out of favour when you were not invited. You could expect to be shot or transported to a Gulag within days.

One evening Stalin did not invite any of his key associates. They all assumed that they were about to be liquidated. When nothing happened a day later they got someone to go into Stalin's room only to discover that he had a stroke of some kind and was lying unconscious in a puddle of his own urine. They did nothing at all, they just let the man die.

Stalin's death indicates that it does not matter how much control the self seeks to exert over the other, the other, life, will eventually produce a set of circumstances that will make the self absolutely beholden to the other. This eventuality manifests what is the fundamental truth in any case. At this point the implications of having made the other deeply hostile to the self are catastrophic for the self. The only other alternative I have to being opposed to the other is to set myself up as allied to the other.

How do I escape the nightmare of being opposed to the other and demonstrate to myself that I exist as part of a continuity, of which I am just a small part; that the other and I are on the same side?

I escape by not acting on the basis of my own self interest. I act on the basis of the interests of the other. Every time I act on the basis of the interests of the other I transcend myself, because I am now saying to myself that I don't have to look after myself. There is a super-ordinate continuity, there is a vastness of which I am a part of and when I act on the basis of the other I am allied to that vastness. An appropriate metaphor for this is an organic one. Your liver produces stuff which is good for everything else in your body, not just your liver. Your liver doesn't exist for itself. Your liver exists for the rest of the body, your heart and every other organ; it does not exist for itself. If it were conscious it would not act in its own interest. It produces that which every other organ in the body requires and when it does that, there is an overall state of wellbeing that the liver also benefits from.

Should the liver consider itself to be cut-off from the rest of the body, it would die. If the liver sought to exist as an individual, it would die as it cannot exist independently. When you give, you become part of a super-ordinate continuity that subsumes you. When you act for other than you, you confirm a wholesomeness which sustains you too.

You tell your inner core, the root of your being, that you don't exist as an individual by acting consistently with the best interest of the other in the situation that you are in, and by doing that consistently. Every time you do that, you are sending a deeper message to yourself: 'I know I do not exist as an individual. I exist as part of a continuity that subsumes me, therefore, I do not have to look after myself. The other looks after me. My role is to look after the other. My role is not to get anything, it is to give something.'

Clearly the effect of this on the world is benign. When you consistently act on the basis of the best interest of the other you will find a spontaneous order manifesting. This is because the other is no longer hostile towards you: it is on your side. In other words, what exists between you and other isn't conflict and hostility, it is harmony and orderliness.

That orderliness will be reflected in your physical environment. There will be a sense of order which will exude from you. The effect of this is that you don't require to be served, and you don't leave disorder in your wake that somebody else has to pick up.

19. There can be no benevolent intention without the affirmation of a greater and absolute continuity that subsumes the self and the other. The loss of conditionality implied by acting with benevolent intention is, therefore, simultaneously the process whereby the self is sublimated into this higher order continuity. The extinction of the self in the process of serving the other establishes a higher order subject that subsumes both self and other. This higher order subject is not in the world. The world is in it.

We have concluded that every time I act in the best interest of the other I transcend myself. The effect of this is that the apparent boundary between self and other becomes less distinct, it becomes thinner. Eventually this progresses to an experience, which the Sufis refer to as annihilation. In this state the boundaries of the self cease to exist. The self becomes one with the other.

This state of oneness is not only a linguistic device. It is something which is experienced firsthand. When you drop into the nothingness behind your eyes you discover a state that is profoundly connected with everything else in ways that you cannot account for rationally. When you go to the depths that your attention functions from, you find that all phenomena that you can perceive are perceived in a matrix, like a bubble, that is encapsulated by that emptiness. In this sense the seen does not encapsulate the seer. The seer encapsulates the seen.

How can we even remotely begin to compare the one who is in the world with the one who has the world within him? This is like comparing a gnat with a colossus, they are incomparable. So the prize that is at the end of the journey of escaping your individuality is an experience of vastness, of incalculable and ecstatic connectedness, which, is in the deepest sense, an end in itself. All other ends have as their purpose this end. This end in itself is, therefore, the zenith, the pinnacle of human experience. This is why we have been created and everything else is a shadow show. The other most extraordinary thing about this is that we all have access to this. This is the human potential. This is the profound truth about who we are. This is the highest experience and it knows no hierarchy, it is not reserved for the privileged.

The pathway to achieving this zenith, is a path of service. It is a path engaging the thick of the world, the guts of the world, with the intention to make the world that we are in a better place. It is not ascetic. It is not withdrawal.

Now, more than ever, this approach is what the world needs. The world does not need any more ethereal mystics. That is not the calling we have. What the world needs now are more people who are profoundly concerned with their immediacy. It is my immediacy. How can I make my immediacy better? How can I serve the people around me, the people in my immediate circle?

20. The more malevolent a person is, the more they will experience the other, and the good auspices of the other, to be discontinuous with the self. The malevolent self is fundamentally in a win/lose competition with the Totality of the Other.

The more I think I exist as an individual, the more I will experience that which is good for them to be bad for me, and, therefore, what is good for me has to be bad for them. Because I have a fundamentally competitive mind-set, I am in a win/lose discourse with the people around me. I don't experience myself to be connected, that there is an energetic relationship between me and the world, that there is a flow; I exist separately as an object.

When I exist as an object the problem is that only one object can occupy a given space, at a given point in time. Two objects cannot occupy the same space which means while I consider myself to exist within my boundaries as an object, I become competitive by definition. For me to be, you cannot be. For me to be, I have to push you out of the way. There can only be one who is significant here. So the more malevolent I am, the more I will experience what's good for you is bad for me, and what's bad for you is good for me.

The real sadness of this is: why am I so competitive? Why am I trying to muscle in and get you to recognize me? It is because in my heart of hearts I actually want to be connected. I want to be recognized. I want to be loved. But how am I pursuing this sense of arrival, connectedness and being affirmed by the other? To do this by competing produces exactly the opposite effect.

When I compete with you I want affirmation from you, but I try to get this by putting you down, demeaning you. As soon as I say my significance is based on your insignificance, it means that in order for you to see me as being significant I am going to make you small.

This does not warmly dispose you towards me. It upsets you, which means you now have exactly the same intent towards me, to demonstrate just how significant you are and what a rat I am. So this desire I'm pursuing, to get your affirmation and love, if I compete, I end up with exactly the opposite. The chalice that I'm drinking is filled with dust, it doesn't nurture, it chokes.

We have created this bizarre quandary so that we can achieve connectedness. This connectedness is not the product of being seen, it is the product of seeing. It is not to be found by pursuing significance, it is to be found by granting significance.

People love those who find them interesting. If you deal with another person not on the basis that you are the significant one in a conversation, but that they are the significant one, people become deeply enamoured with you. People love no one more than the person who finds them genuinely significant and interesting. If you cultivate the habit of granting significance to the other in every situation that you are in, you will discover that they will also find you enormously attractive. They can't get enough of your company.

21. The Totality of the Other presents itself as vast, majestic and unassailable next to the apparent smallness and insignificance of the self. The attempt of the malevolent self to bend the world to its will is therefore fundamentally futile. When the gnat irritates the giant long enough it gets swatted into oblivion.

As a species, it is essential that we understand the meaning of this postulate. We cannot continue doing the horrendous ecological damage to the world that we're in. The party is not going to last. At some point the world is going to react and it will react in a way we can't even begin to imagine. We will not get away indefinitely with what we are doing. We will not get away with continuously shaking our little fists at existence saying, 'We are in charge!'. It is not sustainable. You don't get away with being an annoying little pest in the company of giants indefinitely. It is better that we learn not to pester the giants.

We do this by acting in the best interest of the other in every situation we are in. In every situation, we grant significance to the other and we make our own significance irrelevant. In every situation, we act on the basis of what's helpful to the other, not helpful to ourselves. In every situation we listen rather than talk. In every situation, we get up and serve, rather than expecting to be served. We wash the cup, rather than expecting the cup to be washed for us. The more profoundly we do this, the more we befriend the giants. The less we do this, the more irritating we become and hasten our hour of reckoning.

22. We either give in to the process of submitting the self with good grace, or, we are crushed into submission by the Totality of the Other. Either way the self is destined for extinction.

The self has been created for extinction - not death - extinction. The self will be obliterated. It will be rubbed out as if it was not. The self I am referring to here is our persona, this idea that we exist as an individual. This does not refer to the perceiver, the observer who looks through the mask of the persona.

We have two choices in the face of impending extinction. We can dance, and in the process of dancing we experience that who we thought we were, is not who we actually are. You aren't this individual. You are a far bigger thing that flows through your individuality. When this is the case, the loss of your individuality that death implies is neither catastrophic nor unpleasant. It is deeply gratifying.

The other choice is that we insist that we exist as an individual, in which case your extinction will be horror. The extinction of your individuality, identity and persona is not negotiable. Extinction is your lot as an individual creature, like it is for every other individual creature. It is not negotiable. The only thing that is negotiable is your good grace in the process. So, if you act consistently with the insight that you don't exist separately, then you become part of something which is bigger than you and which cannot die; which doesn't become extinct because it is the One Life from which all life comes.

It is very interesting that some religions describe hell as a fire. Further, it is a fire which perpetually burns off your skin only for it to be instantly replaced. Without going into a debate about the nature of the hereafter, this is a very useful metaphor.

There are no clocks in the grave. There is no metronomic measure of seconds. That belongs to the realm of the living. The final moment of your life is the final moment. It does not have a moment behind it. It becomes a perpetual continuity, it has escaped time. It is no longer in time. There are no clocks. When you die, when you are finally rubbed out, time ceases for you, which means that one moment is an eternal moment.

When you insist that you exist as an individual your death will be experienced as a perpetual burning off of your boundaries, your skin, because at the moment of death you escape time. If stepping into that eternal moment is experienced as a horrifying burning away of your boundaries, that horror does not have a punctuation point behind it. Eternal horror. You have a choice about that eternal moment. It can either be deeply affirming, or like a perpetual extinction, a perpetual burning away of your skin, the boundary which separates you from the world. Horror upon horror!

Constantly acting with the intent to serve is, therefore, about practising for an eloquent death. We need to remind ourselves, however what we have discovered about the intent to serve thus far: There are two ways of trying to maintain the boundaries of the self.

The one is to dominate and the second is to appease. The transactional essence of domination is 'I'm here to get. Shut up and give me what I want. I will brutalize you to suit my own ends.' The transactional patterning of appeasement is 'I give to get.' It therefore has as its essence manipulation, and the problem with manipulation is that it is deeply sleazy.

If you experience somebody trying to dominate you, you resist them and this is a natural reaction, because nobody likes to be dominated. When you experience someone manipulating you, not only do you resist them, but you will actually counter-attack. You seek to do them deep injury because manipulation actually has two injuries. Not only are they trying to get something out of you, but they are treating you like a fool in the process. So there are two injuries here.

You resist me when I'm dominating you and I make you deeply hostile to me when I am manipulating you. That's when people start loosening the wheel nuts on my car - metaphorically - or they start slipping strychnine in my tea, which are both perfectly legitimate strategies for dealing with my deeply unspeakable behaviour. Serving the other, therefore, does not mean appeasement. Serving the other doesn't mean to do things just so that they think you are nice, because that is 'giving to get'.

Giving to give means I do what is appropriate in the best interest of the other in the situation that I'm in. The best interest of the other might be a terrible confrontation that they are not going to like. Very often, when you do what is appropriate in order to be helpful to the other person, you do things to them that they find offensive at the time. Nobody likes being sorted-out. But sometimes people require sorting-out. The appropriate thing to do isn't to always appease and be nice. In my experience, relationships based on appeasement often end up in deep alienation.

Very often the deepest relationships you have are the ones that you really have to struggle with initially. They weren't easy. They were battles. These relationships are often the most useful relationships, because they enable transformation.

So being here to serve the other doesn't mean appeasement. It is doing the right thing, in the best interest of the other in the situation that you are in, whatever that means. If that means a confrontation, it is a confrontation. If that means kindness, it is kindness.

As we discovered before, acting generously in a situation that requires courage is called cowardice. This is taking. Similarly, when you are courageous in a situation that requires generosity, this is selfishness. This is also taking. But actually the worse of the two is not being courageous when the situation demands it. This is the situation that tests you most deeply. In a sense, it is easy to civilize a bully; it is a lot more difficult to get some steel into the spine of a coward.

In all of this, the question may be raised, how do I know where to confront or where to walk away? I suspect that the criteria that are operative are unique for each individual life, and in that sense this is a skill you learn by trial and error, except to say the following: If you have gone into the situation asking yourself what would be helpful to this person or this situation right now, you may not necessarily do what is appropriate, but at least you are attempting to do so. We will explore this more in the next section.

Growth

Maturation is a process, and like any process it is concerned with an incremental progression from a beginning to an end. It happens step by step. Each step of the journey has the same structure. The degree to which you deal with the world on the basis of wanting to get something out of the world, is the degree to which the motive you are taking into the moment will fail in the fullness of time. In the fullness of time everything that you do to achieve an outcome in your interest will be brought to failure, and it will be brought to failure by the other. The house you build, will collapse.

When you do that which is appropriate, the effect is transformative for both the self and the other. This implies that when the outcome of an action is destructive to either the self or the other, then the act was not appropriate. That this happens is inevitable, because we very often do not see the situation as it is. We impose our own conditional motive on it. When the outcome of an action is destructive, it enables a review of one's motive, which allows us to clarify it.

With hindsight, what was appropriate for the other in the situation is normally very clear. At the time, however, our appraisal of the situation can be clouded by our conditionality getting in the way. But we still somehow need to engineer something out of this. So, the good news is that it is better to act anyway, because even if it is wrong, you will always find something to learn.

In the fullness of time, it will become apparent to you how you should have engaged or disengaged. Failure, therefore, enables you to investigate the domain of your conditional motive. So, with the intent to serve, even failure and suffering can produce affirmation as its end. The affirmation is that you learn to scout the boundaries of your own conditionality, and when you do that, you learn the structure of your ego, of the illusion that you exist as an individual.

23. Because a process separates birth from death, it indicates that growth or the transmutation of intent happens incrementally. Each incremental step of change has the same basic structure. The self presents the other with behaviour based on malevolent or conditional motive. In the fullness of time the other confronts this behaviour and the self is presented with failure. This failure necessitates a review of motive by the self.

An infant is here to get unconditionally. An infant is like an emperor. The world is there for them, because they are helpless and, therefore, other has to look after them. At first this is appropriate, which is why good parents are indulgent toward infants and acquiesce to their demands.

Over time, however, the infant is no longer that helpless, and the brazen attitude of 'I'm here to get, unconditionally', gets seen as irksome and inappropriate. Incrementally and increasingly the other resists this behaviour. The parent does not necessarily come running when there is a demand.

This resistance has a constructive outcome. Over time the young Napoleon realises that he cannot just demand or take, he has to be nice, he has to give something to get out of the other what he requires. The behaviour of the adult creates the resistance which then forces him to review his motive. So there is a new patterning and that new patterning is 'I give in order to get'. This happens because the older patterning 'I'm here to get' was resisted.

The fundamental nature of 'I give in order to get' is manipulation. As we argued previously, manipulation produces two injuries to the other: not only do they see that are you trying to get something out of them, but they also experience that you are treating them like a fool. At this point people by and large get really angry. You get a much stronger reaction. It is that reaction that creates the condition by which you once again have to review your intent.

In other words, each moment of growth has the same structure. We want to do what is good for ourselves, for our immediate benefit and interests. The other reads that intent and over a period of time it brings that intent to failure. That failure enables the self to review the self 's intent.

With each moment of growth, you take into the world a conditional motive, an outcome, that you are trying to produce in time. That intent is brought to failure and there is a review of intent, which results in going through a more complex strategy and further delaying gratification. This process continues until the self completely foregoes any intent to produce outcomes, delaying gratification indefinitely.

At this point, the purpose is no longer the outcome; it is the process of doing what is appropriate. The usefulness of the disaster is that you can revisit your intent, and that is the journey of life. Take any intent, a conditional motive, into life, and life will bring that intention to failure. The other, normally other people, bring that intention to failure, so that you have to revisit your intent. This revisiting of intent produces an incremental change. It produces the moment of growth.

24. The nature of the resistance, which the self experiences from the other, is appropriate to the level of maturity of the self. In its most infantile state the self is here to get unconditionally. The other resists this brazen lack of consideration and the self realises that it has to appease the other in order to get what it wants. It therefore 'gives in order to get'.

The infant's view is 'If I'm hungry, I'm hungry now. You must fix me now. Not later. Now!' So, infants do not delay gratification. They want it now. They want to get unconditionally. Over a period of time the infant realizes, 'I've got to be nice to them to get what I want so I have to be a bit more subtle about this.' The story of my oldest son's toddler years comes to mind: his name is Khalil.

When Khalil was toddling I always used to bring him a sweet back from work because he used to react so nicely. I would come up the garden path with a sweet in my hand, he would come waddling up, grab my hand, kiss me and we would be a messy happy couple by the time I got to the front door.

One day I had a day from hell at work and I forgot the sweet. So he sees me walking up the garden path without a sweet in my hand, instantly I changed from being the best thing he'd ever known to being the most repulsive thing on the planet. He threw himself on the ground. He screamed his lungs out because I had the cheek to forget his sweet! Now this drama carried on for a little while and then at some point I realized I was allowing myself to be pushed around by a two-year old! So I said to myslef, 'To hell with this. This is not going to happen!' I decided I would not bring him sweets anymore.

The moment I made that intention, he seemed to intuit this and his whole approach to me changed.

The next time I came home without a sweet he smiled at me and hugged my leg and you could see that he had worked out something in his mind. He'd worked out, 'If I scream at him now, tomorrow I don't get a sweet. If I want a sweet tomorrow, better I give him a hug today.' So he delayed his gratification by going through a little bit of a dance. As we mature that dance gets longer and longer, because by tomorrow I discover that he's manipulating me by being charming, until he decides, 'time to engage another strategy'.

We go through increasingly complex strategies to get what we want, but in the fullness of time that strategy is still brought to failure. So the issue of the maturation of our intent is also simultaneously a process of being able to increasingly delay gratification, until we get to the point where we are able to forego gratification, indefinitely.

The structure of human life is the maturation of intent. It doesn't matter whether you are a man from Beijing, who singularly pursues material success, or a deeply spiritual monk in Lhasa. The same rules of intent govern every life. When you demand brazenly, people start to resist you. When you manipulate the people around you, eventually they will want to break your legs.

25. 'Giving in order to get' is about manipulating the other in order to achieve an end that the self would construe as beneficial to the self. The other disables every transaction based on this intent. Every time a transaction of this nature is disabled, the self attempts a more sophisticated strategy in order to gain control over the other. The increase in sophistication of these strategies amounts to an increased preparedness of the self to delay gratification.

26. Growth is therefore about a sublimation of intent.

I would like to use the growth of a tree as a helpful metaphor to explore the issue of the sublimation of intent. What is initially the seed is always being drawn up into a higher way of being. The seed doesn't stop being a seed and then tomorrow it's a sapling. It is not an on/off thing. It transmutes incrementally. What is in the seed transmutes its nature. From within, it transforms to become a sapling. The seed has been encoded with a simple set of rules that can broadly be described as the following: when presented with sunlight, water and the right soil conditions, push away from gravity toward the light. In a sense, the seed reads the code, it sees the conditions for what they are, and then acts appropriately in that situation. It does not have an idea of what the outcome of a mature tree will look like, but it does not need to.

All it does is act appropriately to the moment, and over time, the outcome of a majestic tree manifests. By responding to its own code, its inner sense of transactional correctness, each stage of the tree is drawn up into a higher form of itself. One could refer to this process as sublimation.

To further expound on the sublimation of intent, I would like to use the 'Six Aspirations' as found in 'Intent'.[1] The First Aspiration, of the infant, is 'happiness is a full maw and an empty bowel'. Simply put the code being followed is: **Full belly = Contentment.**

Very quickly, however, the infant realizes that other people have the power to withhold what makes it happy. The strategy to produce contentment, therefore, becomes a bit more complex. The self realises at this point, that a precondition to getting from the other what you want from them is to control the other.

It is as if the infant say to themselves: 'I've got to get command over them. When I get command over them, control over them, I get them to give me a full belly and, therefore, I become contented.' The strategy to pursue fulfilment therefore becomes a bit more complex: **Command over the other = Full Belly = Contentment.**

If we return to the metaphor of the tree there is a point where the sapling is neither seed nor tree. Soon after having sprouted there are still very evident vestigial signs of the cotyledons of the seed on the stem. Very quickly these vestigial attributes atrophy and get drawn into the stem, so that at some point there is no sign of them and all one sees is the state of the sapling.

Applying this observation to the sublimation of intent would imply the following: In the transition between the First and the Second Aspirations the code of intent is: **Command over the other = Full Belly = Contentment.**

This then sublimates. It becomes fully the next stage when the vestigial part of the previous intent, namely the intent to fill the belly, is fully sublimated into the aspiration to gain control over the other. The Second Aspiration therefore reads: **Command over the other = Contentment.**

With the Third Aspiration the self realises that the self has no command over the other, until the other sees the self as being significant. The desire to pursue significance is first manifest in strategies to appease the other, as is the case with pre-teen children. This, however, eventually also transmutes into the brazen competitiveness of the adolescent. In the transition between the Second and Third Aspirations, the code of intent is: **Significance from the other = Command over the other = Contentment.** It is fully sublimated in the adolescent, who intends simply: **Significance from the other = Contentment.**

The competitiveness of the Third Aspiration presents the adolescent with a new set of problems. The intent of all competition is to win. The aim of winning is to win the love, admiration or favour of the other. For the self to win, however, the other has to lose. This means the self puts the other down in order to be loved by and affirmed by the other.

In actuality, one rarely gets any affirmation from the other by putting them down. More often than not one solicits real hostility. The pursuit of significance, which is, therefore at the root of the Third Aspiration, generally does not earn the affirmation the adolescent is after, it earns ridicule and hostility.

The adolescent begins to intuit that being seen as significant is not about competing with the other; it is about co-operating with the other. You have to genuinely intend to scratch their backs before they will scratch yours. Intent has now shifted again. In the transition between the Third and Fourth Aspirations, the patterning is: **Co-operation with the other = Significance from the other = Contentment.**

This patterning sublimates into the Fourth Aspiration, the aspiration of healthy and properly adjusted adults: **Cooperation with the other = Contentment.**

From within its own logic this Fourth Aspiration produces yet another contradiction: I cooperate in order to make sure that my back still gets scratched, but it is not real cooperation, because cooperation is only cooperation when there is a genuine unconditional intent to be of service to the other person. Quid pro quo is not about genuinely being of service to the other, it is a more subtle form of manipulation. This becomes apparent when the issue of 'balance' comes under review: 'How much have you given me for what I have given you?' In our society marriages rarely survive the mid life crises of either of the parties involved. The reason is that the self feels that the price that was asked in this co-operative venture, called marriage, was too high. The self feels that it has pulled the short end of the stick, that what the other reciprocated was not equal in value to that which the self gave. At this point the self turns to drink and/or the marriage dissolves, unless the self comes to the conclusion that war with the other will continue while we are keeping accounts. The reason for this is that these accounts are always the accounting of apples and pears. What is the relative value of me going to work against her looking after the kids? It is impossible to say. There cannot be real co-operation while we are keeping accounts.

Real cooperation can only work when the self is unconditional with regard to the contribution that needs to be made. Successful marriage is not about give and take, it is about give and give. Most of us spend the first two decades of our life as householders iterating the same lesson: In every clash the hostility only really abates when the self has truly understood that unconditional service to the other, is really what co-operation with the other is about. In the transition between the Fourth and Fifth Aspirations, the pattern of intent is therefore: **Service = Cooperation = Contentment.** This sublimates into the Fifth Aspiration: **Service = Contentment.**

The flaw in this pattern of intent becomes apparent when one considers the intent to serve. The intent to serve the other is still conditional, because it is still concerned with producing outcomes, although the outcomes are benign because they are deliberately in the interest of the other. I bring my wife a pill so that her head feels better. I do the dishes to get the kitchen clean. I pay the college fees so that my child can have an education.

We are genuinely seeking to make things better for the social other, forgetting that the whole theatre is encapsulated by the Totality of the Other, in the face of which nothing will be sustained. No matter how benign the outcome is, in the fullness of time, all things done to produce outcomes will fail. If the headache is not going to get the spouse, then the heart attack will. At some point the very kitchen that I am standing in will be a wilderness and the child that I am educating will die. It may take a few decades, but their death is inevitable. In the face of time, all human endeavour is deeply futile.

Imagine a fantastically wealthy man in Baghdad before the Mongol invasion. He gives huge sums to the building of mosques, he subsidises several caravanserai, and personally provides a pension to all the widows in his neighbourhood. What a noble man! What a fabulously benign use of his wealth, a medieval Bill Gates. And then the Mongols invade and burn down the entire city!

This is the human condition. The Mongols are always there. There is always some barbarian waiting to despoil the fields. No matter how benign the outcome, anything done for an outcome is futile in the fullness of time. This insight produces a spiritual crisis which amounts to a complete abandonment of all conditional motive, no matter how benign. This abandonment also implies a complete surrender of self. In the transition between Fifth and Sixth Aspirations, the patterning of intent is, therefore, initially: **Unconditional surrender of self = Service = Contentment.** This then sublimates to the Sixth Aspiration: **Unconditional surrender of self = Contentment.**

The Sixth Aspiration amounts to a radical shift of attention from outcome to process. The fruits of the aspiration are therefore the security, fulfilment, contentment and harmony that we have associated with full maturity previously.

Sublimation is therefore the process whereby one state transmutes into the next. When applied to the process of the maturation of a person, the thing being sublimated is their intent. Intent transmutes organically, because of the norms that govern the interaction between the self and the other. Intent is moulded by the way in which the other puts pressure on the self and responds to the intent of the self. In summary the Six Aspirations outlined above are:

First Aspiration:
Full belly = Contentment.

Second Aspiration:
Command other = Full belly = Contentment.
Therefore: Command other = Contentment.

Third Aspiration:
Significance from other = Command other = Contentment
Therefore: Significance from other = Contentment.

Fourth Aspiration:
Co-operation = Significance from other = Contentment
Therefore: Co-operation = Contentment.

Fifth Aspiration:
Service = Co-operation = Contentment
Therefore: Service = Contentment.

Sixth Aspiration:
Unconditional surrender of self = Service = Contentment
Therefore: Unconditional surrender of self = Contentment.

27. In the process of growth, the child is introduced to the social order when it discovers that it is discontinuous from the other. This discovery is simultaneously the first apprehension of the capacity of the other to withhold the good auspices of the self, and the birth of the intent to bend the other to suit the design of the self. The core of this intent is about the managing of predictable outcomes beneficial to the self.

The genesis of the intent to manage outcomes in the interest of the self is the genesis of a social persona; the process of becoming an individual. A young infant's experience of life is undifferentiated. They are connected to all things. They do not know where their mother ends and where the self begins, because there is no experience of separateness.

The reason for this is that there is very little delay between need and gratification. They experience a discomfort and scream, and immediately something warm gets put into their mouth. There is very little to suggest that the warm liquid coming into the mouth is separate from the screaming. It is one continuous thing.

At some point, however, the self perceives that the self is not continuous with the other. The self perceives that the self is separate. There is a split. I don't have control over you. You aren't part of me like my hand is part of me. There is a gulf, a chasm, between self and other. The discovery of that chasm, the split between self and other, is the birth of the ego, persona or self. There is a sense that what has been discovered is not a real thing, it is really a convention. For the self to exist separately from other, the self has to assume a boundary. That boundary is not felt as much as inferred from the way in which the self and the other interact.

One way of looking at the persona is that it is the way in which the self claims significance, claims to stand out, claims to be observable by others. At the beginning, when we are continuous with the world, we experience the world as one big subject, one big experience from the inside. When I start experiencing myself as existing separately from the world, that's when I start also experiencing myself as an object. In other words, I am something that I can see.

A young infant cannot recognise themselves in a mirror, then one day, as they get older, they can. An infant relates to themself not just as an experiencer but as an object, as an experiencer. Something seen and not just a seer. This genesis of the ego is also the genesis of the illusion that we exist as one that is seen, as an object, as something which is significant, as something that stands out.

As we mature we become increasingly confused with regard to who we really are. We think we are the convention. We think we are the image in the mirror. This attempt to find ourselves in the image is increasingly futile, like a dog trying to catch its own tail. The self does not exist as an object. You cannot find the observer by turning it into an observation. Who is the observer, actually? Who is this being who looks through your eyes that has a face, called Tom or Jill or Amina? Who is the 'looker'? This is not an object. Pure subject isn't object. It is not something looked at. It is always the looker. This illusion that the subject is an object, a person, is the entrance fee we have to pay to become a person among people.

Our ability to manipulate language is based on the split between subject and object. All languages share that as the fundamental rule - subject and object are different, self and other are different. All social interaction is a language of sorts, all cultures are a language of a kind. They are all rooted on the premise that the self is discontinuous with the other.

Our alienation is what introduces us as a person to other people. There is a point when the infant starts to respond to their name. When that happens they no longer experience themselves as connected to the other. They now know that they are an individual person, they have an identity that can speak back. They become introduced to the community of people. This exile from a deep connectedness with the Totality of the Other is the first introduction to the community, the band of cohort members, the co-travellers.

The point being we are not alone in all of this. How would we be able to mature our intent, in terms of the rules that we've outlined above, if we put ourselves in a place where nobody ever resisted us or confronted us? Intent cannot mature like that. If we went and sat in pristine conditions, where everything was always looked after, where we didn't really have to do anything or talk to anybody, then what conflict would there be that forced us to revisit our intent? Even monastic organizations, like a monastery, are communities. The purpose of that community is the maturation of the intent of the self.

We don't mature without the intense rubbing of discomfort from having to live with other people. The notion that the self exists as separate from other is, in the deepest sense, an illusion, but this illusion has a purpose. The illusion of separateness from other also precipitates the need for other. This need for other produces the dance with the other, that we call the maturation of intent.

The first step in the dance is the assumption that we exist separately, as objects. Over time the pattern that unfolds is the sublimation of intent. The outcome of that pattern, in the fullness of time, is that the self discovers that the very first assumption was false. The very first assumption that made the whole drama start, that the self is separate from the other, is not true. There is no discontinuity between self and other. Rediscovering the essential continuity between the self and the Totality of the Other is redemption and liberation in essence.

The assumption that the self and other are discontinuous is the first cause of our suffering. It is the first discontinuity or lack that produces all other lack, all other suffering. It follows that the loss of the sense of existing separately from the other is also the end of all suffering.

If the self and the Totality of the Other are essentially continuous, it implies that they are the same: that by being part of the macrocosm the self is the macrocosm. In a sense there is only one observer, one looker, and each individual life is the mechanism whereby that which is seen is apprehended by that which is seen.

For example, if I go to a brand new city where I have never been before, I am initially confronted with the problem of getting to know the place. To get to know the place I am going to have to do a lot of walking around, looking at the city from many angles, and every time I look at the city from a different angle, I get a different view. When I have eventually done this three or four hundred times I get a total view of the city. I can claim to know the city.

If the subject is deeply the same as the Totality of the Other, it means that the subject is that which the Totality of the Other views itself. The individual is the vantage point from which the Totality of the Other views the city of its own nature. Each individual life is the Totality of the Other, finding another perspective on its own reality.

Our alienation is purposeful. Everything associated with our alienation is purposeful, including the implied misdoing and predatory behaviour. In a sense our lives are designed in such a way that we are lost so that we can be found; we are in exile so that we can come home. The route out of exile is to behave in a transactionally correct way to the best of our ability.

If we contend that all suffering has its genesis in the assumption that the self exists, it may seem that the purpose of the higher development of the self is to annihilate the persona or ego. In a sense this is true, but one has to see the entire journey as necessary. It is the necessary condition to deliver the self to the point where the self can witness the Totality of the Other. That which is made to be seen loves to be seen, from every conceivable vantage point. Some individuals inhabit a vantage point which allows them to see that which is majestic, others have a predilection for beauty. What they are looking at is the same Other, just from different vantage points.

Each individual, each ego, has a purpose, which is unique. That purpose is not a purpose in doing, it is a purpose in seeing, in witnessing. To maintain this vantage point of observation, however, requires alienation and suffering, and in the face of this suffering it is tempting to tear down the façade of the ego. We do not need to do this.

The same donkey, called the persona, that lead us into exile will lead us home. It is programmed to follow its nose in the direction of transactional correctness. When it follows its nose in that direction its intent is sublimated. It becomes sublime. It transcends the brutality of its genesis, to become subtle beyond expression, transcendent of its individuality.

28. As the self matures, there is a growing insight that vanquishing the other destroys the source of the contentment of the self. There is an understanding that the self cannot achieve peace with the social other in the absence of a negotiated settlement with the social other.

This postulate allows us to summarise the key element at issue as the self engages the other. The immature person tries to get the social other under their command, under their thumb. As the person matures they start to realize that there are just too many. The self may be able to dominate this one or that one, but the third and the fourth are not going to be dominated. The insight comes that, at some point, control fails.

Because the middle point of this process is adolescence, understanding the patterning of the intent of the adolescent is very useful, as it puts the key variables that are at issue in stark relief. Moreover, because we are operating within a world view which has enshrined self-interest, the malaise of the adolescent has become the malaise of the age.

The height of our selfishness is found in adolescence. That is the height of our narcissism, the height of our self-importance and seeking significance. But at some point something deeply changes. Suddenly, the person, who previously could only speak about themselves, becomes quite interested in you. It is no longer just them and their opinions. For a moment they are actually quite curious about what you think. One has a sense that this person no longer views themselves as the centre of their universe. This is expressed behaviourally when they are able to cooperate in order to contribute.

This shift happens because the arrogance of adolescence is a tremendously painful place to be in and it's painful for two reasons: it is a very alienated place for the self and it is a very fear-ridden place. If the self is continuously competing, it is necessarily going to be faced with more instances of failure than success. It is not conceivable that one can succeed in every area all the time. This produces an experience of the self which is continuously under attack, in perpetual turmoil.

Not only is the self inwardly in turmoil, but it is constantly embroiled in conflict ridden relationships. The other is deeply at odds with the dominating and competitive self. This state of war continues until the self shifts its intent from taking to giving, producing harmony with the other and contentment in the self.

The Social Order

So far we have been arguing that the intent to serve, or the intent to give, is fundamentally wholesome and transformative for the individual. To put it differently, we have had a look at what it means to pursue the best in oneself and have discovered the root of the matter is in the intent to serve the other unconditionally, in the moment. When the self distinguishes between what is right and what is expedient, and does what is right, the transformation that takes place is in the direction of ascent, the maturation of the self. This also implies that the sublimation of the self is where the boundaries of the self become thinner, and the self becomes more intimately connected with, and allied, to the other.

Our next section explores how this intent to serve impacts on the social order. The fundamental proposition is that the intent to serve not only has a transformative effect on the self, it also has a constructive effect on the world.

29. **The production of surpluses is an economic metaphor for a successful social order. A surplus suggests that the members of that society have produced more than they have taken out. Collectively, they have given more than they have taken.**

30. **The degree to which members of a society are negotiating on behalf of their own interests is the degree to which the society has cancer and is doomed to failure. This is because the intent of the individuals is to succeed at the haggle, in other words, to get as much as they can for giving as little as possible.**

31. A social order may be described as a pattern of transactions between people. If the intent of the average transaction in a society is malevolent, then the society will be fractured, at war with itself and in a state of decay. The degree to which the individual engages each transaction in view of what is correct and benevolent is the degree to which the society is robust and in harmony.

Enterprise is a very accessible terrain for most people to explore the difference between successful or unsuccessful groups. It is, therefore, convenient to begin an examination on successful groups by exploring successful enterprise. In a capitalist view of economy, people more often than not account for successful enterprise on the basis of profit. Successful enterprises produce profits.

From a socialist point of view, talking profits may seem a bit crass, so people prefer to think about successful enterprise as producing a surplus. From one point of view it is really quite irrelevant whether one refers to this as a profit or a surplus, since the thing being referred to is the same.

Both a profit and a surplus only exist because a group of people have worked together in such a way that the total product they made was bigger than what each individual took out. In other words, surpluses are produced by people who are giving more than they are taking. Healthy enterprises are populated by people who are giving more than they take.

This is not just true for businesses. It is true at every level of human endeavour. Wherever you have individuals who are in pursuit of their own interests, you have a fractured social group. Wherever individuals subordinate their interests for the higher good you have harmony and success.

To give a military example, I once did some leadership work with a group of senior officers in the Pakistan Army. What intrigued me about these men was how enthralled they were with al-Qaeda. I found this surprising, because, on paper, al-Qaeda really is no match for the Pakistani army.

At the time, there were over half a million Pakistanis under arms, whereas there were probably no more than five thousand al-Qaeda operatives around the world. The Pakistanis were not conscripts; they were all professionals, very often coming from a tribal background with a very, deep martial tradition. Man for man each Pakistani soldier was both better equipped and better trained than his opponent. The only thing that differentiated them, was the fact that the al-Qaeda operative threw something into the fray that the Pakistani did not: an absolute and maniacal commitment to his cause.

There are many examples in military history of exactly this phenomenon. From a scale as large as the Vietnam war, to one as focused as the battle of Agincourt, it is this 'x-factor', this unconditional commitment of the individual warrior, which wins through in the end. The Soccer World Cup of 2010 in South Africa also provides some great material to demonstrate the case. It was apparent that all the teams that were populated by stars failed. The degree to which the individual was seen to be playing for his own importance and his own eminence was the degree to which the team was unsuccessful. By contrast, in the teams that succeeded, the significance of individual personalities receded in the light of the overall co-operation of the team. Populate a team with significant individuals and you do not have a team, you have a herd of cats. When individuals willingly subordinate themselves, groups succeed.

It is very important that we understand the nature of this willing subordination of self. It is not simply about getting people to knuckle-down under the stated purpose of the group. If one took any enterprise and had all of the employees in the business assemble in a stadium, you would not have the enterprise, you would have a collection of people in a stadium. The enterprise is more than a collection of people. It is a pattern of individual interactions between members of that organisation.

Each of these interactions can have one of two characters. On one hand they could have a fundamentally competitive character. The degree of this competitiveness would be a direct consequence of the degree to which each individual in the interaction engages the other person with the intent to get something out of the interaction, or to succeed themselves. The degree to which this is the case, is the degree to which the group would be fundamentally fractious and require management from without.

On the other hand, a group can have a fundamentally co-operative character based on the degree to which at least one person in the interaction commits to setting the other person up to succeed, rather than to succeed themselves. To return to the soccer analogy, in attack, the whole team commits to setting-up the striker to succeed. In defence the whole team commits to setting-up the goal keeper to succeed. What captivates the untrained eye is the drama involving strikers and goal keepers. The trained eye sees the magnanimity of all the other players who set-up these heroes.

This all goes to demonstrate that, the degree to which individuals in groups subordinate their own interests in pursuit of what's good for the group, is the degree to which groups succeed. By definition, when the individual in the group pursues his own interests, you no longer have a group. The willing subordination of the individual accounts for the success of groups.

There is, therefore, a dual effect when the self acts on the basis of the best interest of the other in the moment; both the self and the social world become more robust, wholesome and successful. The self-serving individual has a competitive world view. They experience the interest of the other as opposed to their own, they inhabit a world of scarcity and ongoing conflict with the other. When a person commits to give, or serve, they experience a co-operative world of abundance. They no longer need to compete with the other because they act consistently with the view that fundamentally, the other's interest is the self's interest.

This suggests that we can look at society as a pattern of transactions, or interactions. I live in a community called Walkerville, in South Africa. If I consider what this community is actually comprised of, it becomes apparent to me that it doesn't exist independently of individual interactions that happen between people on an ongoing basis.

The degree to which each one of those individuals' actions is based on self-interest, is the degree to which the bigger picture of the community will be in conflict, and self-destruct if no outside intervention was brought to bear on the situation. If each individual is trying to act in the best interest of the other in any given situation, then the bigger picture will be wholesome. One would have a community rather than a warzone.

When each individual is acting on the basis of their own interest the only reason things are held together is because there is a super- ordinate control imposed from above. The community gets brutalized into working, because it doesn't work of its own accord. When the children don't get on and they try to kill each other, it requires a draconian parent to pull in the reigns. While we are all behaving like children in pursuit of our own interests we can't be trusted to get on with things. We need to be under somebody's thumb.

When a society works because there is a brutal super-ordinate control, it has no substance. There is no connectivity. There is no glue in each individual interaction. There is no attraction. We have argued that if I act on the basis of what's good for me in the situation, then I'm dangerous to you and you're dangerous to me. We repel each other, we are in conflict.

When I act on the basis of your interests, I am safe from you because you can't manipulate me anymore, and you are safe from me. In other words, we are connected. So if we look at a society as a collection of connections with each individual being like a brick, the cement that holds them together is the intent to serve, the intent to contribute. If the cement between the bricks is wholesome, is firm, then the façade stands. It does not need to be held up by external forces. When there is no cement between the individual bricks, the façade can't stand. Then it requires external intervention, an external control to keep it standing.

32. The pursuit of transactional correctness is simultaneously the path of unfoldment of the individual and the establishment of a legitimate social order. The individual's highest self-interest therefore lies in acting consistently in the best interests of the other.

Transactional correctness means that I attempt to do what is right rather than what is expedient or convenient. So, for example, in each transaction I attempt to be fair with the other person. I do not try to squeeze as much as possible out of them. If I am a boss in a company having to deal with a disciplinary problem, I try to do what is fair, even if that is, in the immediate term, injurious to me or the group. Transactional correctness means committing to doing what is right or just, in the moment, irrespective of outcome.

33. A society based on the pursuit of self-interest will cultivate hostility between the generations, the sexes and between the leaders and the followers.

Any group has potential fault lines. These fault lines are as numerous as the individuals within the group. If there are different races in the group, then there will be a fault line between the races. If there are different generations in the group, there will be a fault line between the generations. If there are different genders in the group, there will be a fault line between the genders, and so on. This is necessarily the case because absolute homogeneity is impossible to establish in a group.

The degree to which each individual in the group pursues his or her own interests, is the degree to which these fault lines will manifest as cracks or tears in the social fabric. So generations will pit against each other, races will pit against each other, neighbourhoods will pit against each other and ethnic groups will pit against each other.

When left ungoverned, societies seem to descend into warzones. We need the police to arrest and lock up those that get out of hand on an ongoing basis otherwise things seem to spiral out of control. This means that the apparent peace that we may see on the street does not mean that people are connected. People aren't connected. The religions aren't connected, the races aren't connected, the genders aren't connected and the classes aren't connected. The whole thing is like a fractured vase that's being held together, bureaucratically, with play-dough. It is just waiting to implode.

34. A person in pursuit of his or her self-interest is fundamentally untrustworthy.

If I act on the basis of what is good for me, when I am in a situation where what is right and what is in my own interest are pitted against each other, I will do what is in my own interest. This means that you cannot trust me. Trustworthiness means that you believe that, when I am faced with a choice between what is right and what is in my own interest, I will do what is right. The extent to which a person consistently acts on the basis of their self-interest is the extent to which you cannot trust that person. We could, therefore, say that the principle attribute of a fractured society is distrust.

The hostility between generations, between the sexes, between ethnic groups and religions will be expressed as distrust between them. A very cursory examination of our global village makes apparent just how ubiquitous this distrust is. It is most evident in the scepticism of authority. This jaundiced view of authority is firstly expressed in a reasonably, widely-held disdain of politicians. To describe someone in an organisational setting as 'politically astute' often means that you have just insulted the person. When used as a verb, the word 'politicking' is seen to be the behaviour of a person who is underhanded, conniving and manipulative.

A further attribute of the distrust of authority is the prevalence of conspiracy theories nowadays. Many people feel that the authority that they see is somehow theatre, that the real authority is wielded from behind the scenes by the bankers, the 'Illuminati', the CIA or some other sinister lot. Often, there is credible evidence for the view being articulated, revelations of the American cold-war interference in the affairs of sovereign developing countries being a case in point. Julian Assange, of Wikileaks', cult-hero status would not have happened if people did not feel that that which was hidden by the authorities had been exposed.

Conspiracy theories are saying you can't trust the world that you see. There is a hidden hand, a malevolent hand behind it all, which is orchestrating all of this. All conspiracy theories are an attribute of a lack of faith in authority. It sees authority as deeply malevolent, so much so that its real designs have to be hidden under a veil of secrecy. This suspicion of authority is quite often extended to the functionaries of the state. When I was eight years old I was joined in a lift by a man, who had the phrase 'I HATE COPS' emblazoned on his T-shirt. I can remember being awfully impressed by this fellow's brazen courage. It was the '60's in South Africa, after all. I do not think, however, that my response was purely an attribute of my dysfunctional background. I have discovered that many people of my generation all over the world shared this intuitive disquiet regarding the functionaries of the law.

35. The degree to which there is an element of unconditional service in the intent of the self is the degree to which the self makes peace with the social order. The attempt to be of service to the other, amounts to the intent to manage outcomes beneficial to the other. While this intent is benevolent, the behaviour that flows from it is still conditional. It is benevolent 'getting to give'.

We have established that the journey of our personal maturation starts off with acting on the basis of our immediate self-interest, as is the case with infants and juveniles. Once you have children, however, and you become a parent, there is no question about who is here to serve who. Infants cannot look after themselves. We get up when it's not comfortable for us and we do the serving. Adulthood is about being here to serve the world around you and the people around you.

You are doing all of this to help them. You feed the child because the child is hungry. You go to work to pay the school fees and the mortgage. This suggests that your behaviour is conditional, because it is about achieving an outcome. The outcome, however is benign. It is for the other, for the social other, more specifically. You are trying to make the world a better place.

Beyond the Social Good

In the process of trying to manage the hunger of the child, it does not seem to occur to you that the belly you are filling is going to one day remain permanently empty. That belly will die. Sitting behind all our good acts in the interests of others is a grand futility. Everything that you do, no matter how well-intentioned, in the fullness of time, will fail by definition, because that's the fate of all phenomenal things. This is not cause for depression, because it enables new exploration.

It implies that serving other people, acting in the best interests of other people, is not the end of the journey, it is a stepping stone. It is something that enables something else. Service of the other is what rescues us from the nightmarish narcissism of adolescence. It is an inevitable step on the journey to becoming unconditional. Serving unconditionally is not about being the one who satisfies other people's hunger, it is to be the one who feeds. Period.

The end is to serve without the intent to produce an outcome. It is your status to serve. That is what it means to do things unconditionally. In other words, we do this because this is our dance with life, our door to something. The degree to which there is an element of unconditional service is the degree to which the self makes peace with the social order, and transcends the social order. The deepest parts of our selves are beyond the social good. We do not only have a relationship with the social other, we have a relationship with the Totality of the Other.

When we act with truly unconditional intent, we are introduced to a new universe - a miraculous universe - a universe where our own inadequacy is part of the overall function. Our inadequacy becomes the platform from which we witness the stupendous way in which it all works, above and beyond our own ability to manage.

36. Preparedness for death implies the capacity to give unconditionally. This implies a fundamental disavowal of any pretence of usefulness or capacity to manage outcomes. 'Giving to give' implies a disregard for outcome, or what is going to be achieved. At this point, the maturation of the self requires a fundamental alienation from the social order, since death is an alienation from the social order.

If dying is the most absolute form of giving, and corpses are fundamentally useless and offensive to other people, it must mean that our highest attributes are concerned with more profound things than being good to other people. We are here to do more than just be good citizens.

Our being is vast. Our inner reality is infinite, ancient and supremely wise. The apex of experiencing this is the moment of death, because death describes the event where you rejoin everything else, you become one with what you came from. As human beings, we are born to grow, to stand out as an individuals, quite separate and distinct from what is not us. We walk around the planet, go on to do something cool for some person and then, at some point, we die.

When I die, all the things that form the platform that enables me to stand out as an individual disperse from me, so that I disappear back into the one thing I came out of. I have come from the oneness that contains all things, and I will go back into the oneness that contains all things. The highest part of me is that oneness that contains all things. This is the destiny I am aimed at. For me to achieve that oneness that contains all things, I have to stop being a person identified with my own name, shape and personal history. I have to disappear. I have to leave the world of men.

The highest aspect of you is death. Death is not social. Death is individual. If somebody rolled a poison grenade through the door that killed us all, we would not have a convivial experience. I could not say, 'John, I can't breathe any more. Are you still moving your feet?' We die individually. The highest aspect of us is aimed at something which is beyond and outside of the social good.

So there is a paradox in this. The paradox is: serve society, serve the other, so that the real secret of existence can happen. The service itself is a means, it is not the end. The service is a means to producing this extraordinary being, who can lose everything, unconditionally, right now, because nothing is done with a thought for the future. Everything is done unconditionally to contribute, in the moment, now.

37. The final fulfilment of the destiny of the individual is, therefore, beyond the social good. In this sense, the successful life is super-ordinate to the social good. The individual is super- ordinate to society. The social order is fundamentally there to enable the individual, not the other way round.

38. Societies that are concerned with the enablement of the individual are fundamentally benevolent. Societies that subordinate the enablement of the individual to the social project are fundamentally malevolent.

When we act in the best interest of the other we have a wholesome society. That intent produces a transformed self that eventually contains the whole universe. While it seems that we are serving society, that we are doing it for the other, we are in fact enabling the best in ourselves. That which is the best in ourselves is vast beyond comprehension. It spans the universe, let alone society.

It appears as if the individual is therefore society, but really it is the other way around. If social conscience is a stepping stone to a higher state of consciousness of the individual, then by definition society is a means, a step, not the end, or the point of the matter. You are not here for society, it is there for you. The individual isn't there for the other, the social other, the social other is there for the individual. It provides the excuse for the individual to act for reasons bigger than the self, and when the individual does that to an extremity the individual becomes the purpose of creation.

This means that the aim of the social order is to enable the individual, not the other way around. The individual isn't the cannon fodder for the social order. As soon as you smell the brutality of an order that's being imposed with an iron fist from above, then know that something is wrong. It cannot be appropriate. Society is supposed to enable transcendental human beings, extraordinary individuals. It is about the individual. It can't be about this drab uniformity, where we all no longer have our own lives, because we are marching to somebody else's drum.

When we give up the busyness of doing things that are concerned with fixing the world, we are introduced to the status of being the one who sees. The one who really sees things as they are sees that whichis stupendous, wondrous and overwhelming. A key ingredient, which catalyses this experience, is the insight into my own inadequacy.

I know inadequacy because I know myself. This enables me to witness the supreme adequacy of the Totality of the Other. It is that Totality which has produced me. I have come from that Totality to be the vantage point from which the witnessing of its stupendous nature can happen. More than being here to do, I am here to see. My seeing is enabled by the inadequacy of my doing. This apprehension happens because I have committed fully to helping my fellow men and failed.

We conclude: If seeing things as they are is not good enough for me, I am not seeing things as they are.

Moses and Pharaoh

All three Semitic faiths share the account of the Israelite exodus from Egypt under the leadership of Moses. This account speaks to the heart of the dilemma of being human in a complex society. We find within us a conflict between two beings: one compliant and risk averse, the other somewhat wilder and thirsting for authenticity. It is this discourse that happens between the soldier and the warrior. The account of the exodus gives us very useful material to examine this conflict.

39. In Semitic mythology this distinction is explored in the account of Moses and Pharaoh. The Pharaonic model subjugates the people to the work of the social project. This project amounts to the construction of the pyramidal mausoleum of the leader. The aim of this mausoleum is to ensure the immortality and eternal aggrandizement of the leader. The people are enslaved to this project, principally, because of their own need for the security of life in Egypt. In the Mosaic model the social project is fundamentally bizarre. It amounts to an aimless wandering through the desert for forty years. This wandering, however, is about enabling a generation of free people. The social project is, therefore, the means to the end of enabling the people, not the other way round. Moses, the leader, never gets to the Promised Land. He is expended in the process of freeing the people from slavery.

Our current take on leadership is informed by our understanding of the purpose of work. Work, from the current point of view, is to do useful things. Those in charge of the society are those who designate what work is useful, and the most useful work is concerned with building things that are impressive - edifices.

In our current age, as in ancient Egypt, the pyramid is the aim of all work. If this is not so in terms of constructing buildings, then it is at least so metaphorically: We have made the pyramidal structure the metaphorical framework for organisational life. When we speak about the structure of an organisation, the image that often springs to mind is a pyramid.

This pyramid has a person at the apex and that person is the hero, orchestrating all the work, and everybody else is subordinate to the purpose of that work. If we look at what happened to the people in Egypt, almost the entire society was enslaved to build this pyramidal structure that was designated as useful by the Pharaoh.

The usefulness of the pyramid was very specific: It was a mausoleum of epic proportions, wherein the Pharaoh would live forever. This suggests that, in a pyramidal, society all work that is designated as useful is actually about the eternal aggrandizement of the one in charge, the leader. When work is designated principally as being about knuckling down and being useful, we have to ask the question 'useful to whom?'

To knuckle down and become useful is to become the foot soldier for the social project, which is concerned with furthering the interests of these iconic figures that have been put in charge; the ones who are on top of the pile. This is the wrong way around. The leader should be there for the people. The people aren't there for the leader.

The leadership of Moses represents something entirely different. First of all, the task is quite bizarre, and in a sense useless and futile. It is about wandering around the desert for forty years. The purpose of this wandering was not to produce anything concrete, like a pyramid. The purpose was to enable a generation of free people: people who were not slaves. The aim of the work, the wandering, was to transform the worker, the wanderer.

This means that the people weren't there for the work. The work (the wandering) was there to enable free people. The object of the work, the object of the struggle, was not to achieve a utopian order. The object of the struggle, was to achieve a free individual. The incidental purpose of work is to do useful things. The essential purpose of work is the transformation of the worker.

In fact, it doesn't matter what the work is. All you know is that you have to work, you have to struggle. The struggle could be completely bizarre, like wandering around the desert for forty years.

One could imagine the conversations:

'So, where are we going now?'
'I have no idea!'

This may seem like absolutely ridiculous work Why? Because the purpose of the work does not seem to achieve anything. The purpose of the work is to transform the self. That is why we work. In the process of doing this, the leader, Moses, does not attain the Promised Land: he gets expended in the process. Far from using people to achieve the leader's end, the leader is used up or expended in the process of enabling their freedom.

So, we are currently looking at things upside down. We are not here for society. Although we say serve, serve, serve the other - understand that the purpose of serving the other is not to fix the other, because the other is made to be fundamentally broken. It is not going to be fixed. The aim is to serve so that you serve yourself empty. Once you have served yourself empty, you have drained it all; you then occupy a place which is preparedness for death. You can describe the preparedness for death as the high point, the most sublime, the most singular achievement of a human life

The utopianism of the modern age does violence to the profundity that the Semitic faiths have brought us. If one examines the Islamic heritage, for example, then the real contribution made by the followers of the Prophet Muhammad was not the buildings, the books, or the institutions and universities. The real heritage was extraordinary people who could make a school under a tree. A school is a place where learning takes place, it is not a building.

The aim of good work is to enable individuals. It is not to build structures, it is not to build edifices and it is not aggrandizement. Making the project the enablement of people rather than aggrandizement certainly feels closer to the self-effacing frugality of the endeavour of the Prophet Muhammad and his early companions.

40. A Pharaonic society, therefore, subordinates the growth of the individual to the social project and the social project is about the immortality and aggrandizement of those in control.

A Mosaic, or prophetic society, applies the social project to the end of enabling free and mature people, and the leadership of this society expend themselves to this end.

41. Correct leadership, therefore, entails understanding that the role of the leader is to serve or care for the followers. This care, however, is fundamentally about the growth of the individual, in other words, cultivating the individual's freedom, maturity and power. It is about cultivating the individual's capacity for unconditional benevolent action. Legitimate leadership is about the care and growth of the follower. Likewise, a legitimate social order is about the care and growth of the individual.

The question may arise 'How does a leader of a society get chosen?' or 'How do you choose a legitimate leader of a group?' Actually, the mechanism whereby a person attains power is not necessarily relevant to understanding what makes power legitimate. It is what the person does with the power that is the point. You can have any mechanism to choose a leader and you could still end up having a self-interested ego-maniac in a position of authority.

I would imagine the Founding Fathers of America were all well-intentioned men. They tried to do what, in their view, was benign and fair, that would put people in charge who would responsibly govern the interests of the people of the United States of America. That same mechanism also put presidents in charge who were, arguably, some of the most dangerous men in history.

It is entirely conceivable that a person, who is a hereditary king can act consistently with being here to serve the people, and we know many stories of hereditary kings where this was the case. On every continent and at every age you will find examples of a hereditary king, or a hereditary chief, who was extraordinary, who demonstrably governed in the interest of the people rather than to get something from the people.

If the problem of legitimacy is how you get power, then what you are doing is replacing a requirement for what makes power legitimate with a rule of succession. A rule of succession is not a model for what power has to do. How you get power is different from what power

has to do. It doesn't matter what the rule of succession is - you can be just or unjust once you have the power. So our current position around democracy and democratic social orders has a naivety to it, because it confuses the idea of legitimacy and legitimate power, with a rule of succession. They are two different things.

I am not suggesting that we should not work. We all need to work, to put a roof over our own heads and then later on to live up to the responsibility of taking care of those near to us. I am suggesting that we need to review the purpose of our work. Particularly, when we get to a point where our achievements seem a bit facile it is helpful to remember that the purpose of work is a transformed self.

At some point we no longer work to earn money. The money may or may not come, but it is not the issue. We work because when we work we change. The purpose isn't the other, or of achieving things in the objective world. The real purpose is a transformation of the subject, the seer, the inner self.

So, this is the insight that the account of the distinction between Pharaoh and Moses makes possible. Pharaoh is about useful work that builds things, but actually that is all just a ruse. In this case the real purpose is entrenching those in charge, forever if possible.

Good work, as a by-product of the process of the care and growth, produces good men and women. When these people work they no longer work to sustain themselves, no more than the wanderers wandered to sustain themselves. Every task in their working day is concerned with perfecting the work of art, called their lives.

Governance

We started with the contention that the issue of intent forms a golden thread for a unified field of theory for all of the Human Sciences. The postulates commenced by examining how the intent to serve affects the individual. We then looked at how the intent to serve affects the transaction between the self and the other and, by implication, how that affects groups. We shall now explore what all of this means for systemic variables, like governance.

42. Legitimate governance is concerned with enabling the best in the citizen. This means that, at the end of a legitimate political establishment, the average citizen will be functioning at a higher level on the continuum of intent than was the case when that establishment came to power. Conversely, illegitimate governance will finish with the citizen functioning at a lower level along the continuum of the maturation of intent than was the case when it started.

Our examination of the story of the Exodus really asks us to consider what the purpose of authority is, and why, if ever, we should submit to it. Subordinating to authority comes at a price, and that price is, by definition, the loss of individual freedom.

In the first instance, if we had absolutely no sense of authority, the human being could not survive. If we look at the relationship between parent and child, then it becomes clear that it is the authority of the parent that brokers the child into being a person among people. If there was no sense of imposition by a powerful other on the life of the child, the child would stay a wolf child, if it survives.

We are designed in such a way that we cannot survive very long without nurturing. It is physically impossible for a human being to survive childhood without an authority, at least without authoritative intervention. Without the imposition of authority in your life and a sense of limitation, you do not develop an ego or persona, you don't develop the first rules of language and you cannot engage with others. The human condition requires power, but as we have described, power or authority has one of two ways of manifesting. It either manifests in a way where the powerless, the subordinated, are here to serve the powerful or the powerful are here to serve the powerless, the subordinate.

Naively put, the account of Moses suggests legitimate power is what happens when the big one is there for the little one and illegitimate power is when the little one is there for the big one. Tyranny is concerned with the weak serving the interests of the powerful. Legitimacy is concerned with the powerful serving the interests of the weak.

If the powerful are there to serve the weak, does that mean that the powerful have to acquiesce to all of the demands of the weak? If the powerful are there to serve my interests, then surely whatever I want they should supply? This is clearly not true if we look at the situation that parents face. A good parent doesn't allow the child to get away with murder, because it is not in the interest of the child. If the parent acquiesces every time the child asks for a sweet, you will have a sick child.

In other words, very often the subordinated experience authority as negating. When that negation is correctly placed, however, it is in the best interests of the subordinate. The powerful are there to serve the weak, the powerless. This service is concerned with empowering the weak, just like good parents turn out well-adjusted adults, not needy and dependent children in adult bodies. In order to achieve this, the parent does not acquiesce to each and every demand of the child.

We demonstrated previously that the empowerment of the human being is about cultivating the intention to serve, because those who are here to give become powerful. We know that if you want something from somebody else, that person's ability to withhold what you want gives them power over you. You become weak and they become strong. If you want to give something to somebody else, they have no power over you.

This means that when you grow or empower someone you are cultivating the propensity to serve. A legitimate political establishment cultivates powerful people who are in the world to serve. An illegitimate, political establishment will produce a population who are needy, weak and whose fundamental, average engagement with the social other is about their own personal interests rather than the intent to serve.

This implies, as is the case with people, that one assesses political establishments by their fruits. A legitimate establishment produces a more generous and serving citizen. An illegitimate establishment produces a more self-serving, corrupt and untrustworthy individual. This suggests that governance in the 20th and 21st Centuries has failed miserably.

It certainly has done so in my own country of South Africa. There is no question about the fact that the average South African today is far more entitled, needier and concerned with what they have to get out of the world than before. This is despite the fact that we have a far more democratic, political process than we had under apartheid. So it is entirely conceivable that an apparently legitimate government, based on a democratic process can constitute an illegitimate, political establishment that produces disabled and dysfunctional people.

43. Illegitimate governments leave the people more greedy, selfish and needy than they found them. Conversely, legitimate governments leave the people more courageous, honourable and generous than they found them.

44. A malevolent social order has a vested interest in the disablement of the individual. It will seek to cultivate neediness, insecurity and conditional behaviour in the individual. It is precisely this behaviour which lays the foundation for its demise.

Brazenly malevolent and tyrannical political establishments have as their primary objective destroying the natural connectivity between people, and to replace that with a loyalty to the state. Some of the attributes of this is are that family members are encouraged to inform on each other, and brazen disloyalty to kin and loved ones is considered praiseworthy and laudable. The aim is to produce compliance in the citizen at any cost.

The effect of this is that, over time, the only initiative that remains in society is deeply malevolent and conniving. People do not serve each other, they only serve themselves. There is no social fabric to speak of. The system only persists because of the draconian control imposed from without.

This draconian control is inefficient and expensive. It amounts to always committing to increasing resources to ensure that you get what you want from the people, because you cannot rely on them to give it. As the Soviet Empire demonstrated, at some point the cost of the control bankrupts the state and it implodes.

The wreckage that remains after the implosion is on two levels: It is firstly at the level of the group or the society, with a system controlled by Mafiosi and fuelled by graft: or worse, it is at the level of the individual. The outlook of the citizen in most former Soviet countries seems bleak, narrow, harsh and pickled in Vodka. These are deeply unhappy people.[2]

This is not to suggest that we should therefore champion capitalist libertarianism. Both the capitalist and the socialist views of the individual are essentially the same: the individual is fundamentally self-interested. The socialists deal with this assumption by controlling the individual. The capitalists, on the other hand, view self-interest as something laudable and encourage it. The effects of this assumption of self-interest are the same.

The disaster brought on by the sub-prime crisis demonstrates the case. Bankers were paid astronomical bonuses for selling mortgages to people, who really could not afford them. These people were themselves lured into these deals in pursuit of ownership. Greed upon greed. In essence, the frenzy of acquisition and accumulation that ensued was founded on the promise to others to pay nothing for something, by those who were frantically trying to get as much as possible for nothing. The result was that burgeoning economies, like the Irish, got reduced to penury within months.

An illegitimate establishment needs weak people and cultivates weakness in people. This weakness is cultivated by encouraging selfish and cowardly behaviour in people. This self-interest causes the demise of the system and destroys the individual, just like cancer. It is never sustainable.

45. The liberal defence of human rights confuses the right of the individual to be enabled with self-interest. It therefore forms part of the ideological justification of a fundamentally malevolent social order.

The powerful are there for the powerless. The parent is there for the child. The parent is there to serve the best interest of the child. The parent is not there to acquiesce to every demand of the child because that is not in the child's best interest. Power is legitimate when it enables and empowers the powerless. With this objective in mind, the powerful may do things to the powerless that the powerless don't like.

The test, at the level of the individual is, did the imposition enable maturity? Did it cultivate a greater sense of focus on your own contribution rather than what you were getting out of the system. As a result of this focus on contribution, is your sense of security, fulfilment, power and harmony less dependent on external conditions? Fundamentally, if power doesn't make you powerful, it is illegitimate. If it solicits the most demeaning and self-serving parts of you, it is not empowering you, it is disabling you.

So, when you have an ideology that says you have rights, ask yourself, 'Where does that right sit?' If I have a right, who owes who? Does the self owe the other or does the other owe the self? Clearly, when I have a right, other owes self. In other words I am constructing a worldview not on what I'm contributing or giving. Rather I am constructing a worldview on what I'm getting.

The defence of my right, and having a political ideology emphasising my right, says to me that it is legitimate for me to construct my engagement with the world on the basis of my right, and what I am getting. In the process I forget that every moment I'm alive, two variables are operative - what I'm getting and what I'm contributing: my right and my duty.

When I focus my attention on what I am getting, I am focusing my attention on what I do not have power over.

In other words, I become weak. When I focus my attention on what I am contributing, in other words my duty rather than my right, I become powerful.

This liberal focus on human rights keeps peoples' attention on what other owes self, and therefore keeps people weak. It sits at the root of the deep victimhood of the 21st century. It is as if everyone has a 'look at what they have done to me' refrain, even the privileged.

46. Making the social project subordinate to the individual does not imply endorsing rampant individualism and self- interest. The generation that fled Egypt found the wandering through the desert fundamentally onerous. Their own freedom meant giving up the collusion of mediocrity that gave them security. In this sense, freedom from tyranny is simultaneously freedom from Pharaonic oppression, and a disavowal of the expectation of security.

This view of legitimacy has a paradox at its root. We have argued that the powerful should serve the powerless. Leaders are there for the people. The parent is there for the child. The teacher is there for the pupil. The coach is there for the athlete. Where you find power, the purpose of that power is to serve the interest of those who are subordinate to the power.

We have also argued that this service is not about confirming and pursuing self-interest - the immediate, rampant, individualistic self-interest of the subordinate, of the powerless. It is exactly the opposite. It is about cultivating the propensity to serve.

We saw that Pharaoh's pyramidal project subordinated the whole of society to ostensibly useful work, but which was actually about creating a mausoleum for the eternal aggrandizement of the leader.

In the case of Moses, the work that was done had no other aim than to cultivate a generation of free people. It was certainly not about creating something useful like a building. The work that was done had the specific purpose to transform the one who was doing the work in pursuit of their enablement and freedom.

The key point about this is that people don't necessarily like it when it is happening to them. The generation that fled Egypt kept on rebelling. They wanted the security of Egypt. They wanted their cucumbers. It was as if they were saying 'What's this crazy stuff, going through the desert?' They did not necessarily enjoy pursuing a project that was not there to get something from them. They found the struggle to become free, onerous.

It stands to reason that it is possible to compel somebody in their own interest. It is only legitimate to compel somebody, however, when it is in their best interest; otherwise the compulsion is tantamount to violent crime. Legitimacy is not about compulsion or persuasion, it is firstly about the intent of the powerful, and secondly, about the skilfulness of the powerful.

The powerful may, with good intent, misapprehend the situation that the subordinate is in and compel the subordinate inappropriately. This is regrettable, but is forgivable. What is unforgivable is when the powerful skilfully fleece the weak. The core variable is not skilfulness, it is intent.

If the intent of the powerful is to create the conditions where the weak will rise to greatness, they will not allow people to act consistently with their own, narrow self-interest. The role of the powerful is to empower the weak. That only happens when the powerful are willing to confront.

From one point of view, it is the subordinate's requirement for security which legitimate leadership confronts. If you have an expectation of security and you feel that you are owed a livelihood, a roof over your head and clothes on your back, then you are constructing your sense of security like a slave constructs his sense of security. You are constructing your sense of security based on an accusation towards the world, what other owes self.

Legitimate leadership enables contributors: people who look at what they are giving, rather than getting. These people do not have an accusation against the world. This is about accountability. If I'm unhappy because of what I'm getting from you, then you are accountable for my state, which means I don't have to do anything.

That is the victim's call - security! 'I don't have to do anything. That is your problem.'

If I'm unhappy, because there is something inadequate about my own contribution, I'm accountable. So, the key issue presently is that we are dealing with a worldview that creates the conditions that people can escape the problem of accountability. They view the other as fundamentally accountable rather than the self.

This sense of not being accountable seriously damages people. It cultivates a climate where expediency reigns: that it doesn't matter that you should do what is appropriate in the situation. It produces people who only do what suits themselves. This speaks to their lowest nature: their laziness and self-serving nature.

47. An enabling social order requires the individual to pursue goals that are greater than self-interest. They are goals that are fundamentally generous in character. Every incremental step of growth implies an incremental shift of intention in the direction of benevolence. This is only possible if the social other holds the individual accountable for the malevolence of their intention.

To repeat the rule: If we construct our lives on the basis of what we want to get from the world we become weak, insecure and discontented; and we are in conflict with the world around us. To suffer this state is clearly not in our best interest. When we construct our lives on the basis of what we should contribute, we then become secure, fulfilled, powerful and in harmony with our world. This is clearly in our best interests.

The critical factor that the other, most specifically the powerful other, brings to bear on us that enables the shift of our attention from getting, to contributing, is to hold us accountable for the malevolence of our intent. More often than not we find this sense of being held accountable objectionable.

Legitimate power does not only hold me accountable. Legitimate power gives me a reason to act for something higher than myself. It gives me a vision. It could be a national vision. For example, as South Africans, we had one for a while: The Rainbow Nation. It was a beautiful thing that we could offer the world, a vision of congruent humanity, cooperative and harmonious humanity, of ubuntu [3]. It was something that 'gave'. It saw a revival during the recent 2010 Soccer World Cup. During the World Cup we were all proudly South African. We were pleased to be the generous hosts to the people of the world. This sense of being host to the people of the world was good for our country and it restored dignity to us as individuals. The last time I was as deeply appreciative of being a South African was when the elections of 1994 successfully subverted a civil war.

Accountability of the Citizen

If a legitimate order has as its project the enablement of mature people, people who accept accountability rather than blame, it follows that legitimate establishments make much of the accountability of the citizen.

48. A social order that does not hold the individual accountable for the malevolence of their intention is fundamentally disabling. Such a society can only cultivate weak, grasping, cowardly and selfish individuals. Such people will be ill equipped to face the most fundamental existential problem, namely the proximity of death.

Death only asks you one question: 'How eloquently can you give or lose everything right now?' Death has absolutely no interest in what you have accumulated in your life. It is exclusively concerned with how eloquently you can lose it all. This is true for every human being, whether you are a Dawkinsesque atheist or a fanatical believer. It is part of the natural order of things that we are all deeply accountable for our capacity to lose, or to give, or serve unconditionally. We are not accountable for our capacity to have accumulated, unless we are executives in a capitalist enterprise.[4]

I develop the capacity to give by living in a social context where my peers and the powerful hold me accountable for my intent. My parents and siblings, compatriots and leaders tell me: 'You cannot do this! This is shameful!'

Because I'm being held accountable for my intent they create the possibility that I start acting with an increasingly higher order of intent. It is a natural process. If we live in a world that is completely laissez faire and nobody may judge me for anything, then how can we play this role for each other? How can we be helpful to each other to face the exam of the Grim Reaper?

Without an engagement with the world that confronts me with my intention, I do not grow. The fundamental mechanism that sits underneath all growth is negation. If I was not rebuked or corrected for my tantrums as a three-year old, I would still tantrum like a three-year old today.

At every level, a higher order of maturity is established because the lower order way of functioning is made dysfunctional by the other. The other confronts you. You are held accountable for your intent. All actions are driven by intentions. That is to say, the value of an action, the significance of an action is judged on the basis of its intent. Accountability is about intent.

49. It is unjust to hold a person accountable if they do not have the means or are not able to make the contribution required of them. A person does not have the ability to contribute if they do not know why or how to make the contribution required of them.

This postulate holds true both for the employee in the organisation and for the citizen in society. It is founded on the insight that to enable or empower somebody means more than to give them a fish; it is to enable them to fish. If you wanted to enable the person to fish then you would clearly have to give the person all the means required to do this. This would include a rod, a reel, a licence, some bait and so on.

All of these things, however, are not particularly useful if the person does not know what to do with them. Further to providing these things you would, therefore, have to teach the person both how to use them, and why they should use them. So, part of enabling someone is to provide them with the means and the ability to do what is required of them.

That said, the means and the ability are not adequate on their own. If, in the process of empowering someone to fish, you also told them that you had a freezer full of fish, and that you would gladly give them one from your freezer, they are unlikely to fish. It suggests that over and above providing people with the means and the ability, empowering them also means, that at some point you have to be willing to tell them to 'starve'. You are willing to hold them accountable for the means and the ability that they have been entrusted with.

When applied to a modern state, in an overall sense, the state's role is to provide the means to enable the citizen, to allow rather than to disallow. The proverbial 'nanny state' which the good citizens of the United Kingdom accused Tony Blair of making, would therefore, be deeply illegitimate. It also suggests that one of the last things that a legitimate government would consider cutting back on would be education.

All of this, however, becomes irrelevant if people are not held accountable for appropriately using the opportunities that the state provides. There is currently an overall climate of licentiousness that pervades modern life, which designates any sense of holding people accountable to the realm of political incorrectness. In South African government schools this is extreme. The degree to which the educational authorities tolerate vandalism of premises, brazen indiscipline by teachers and mediocrity in students is criminally negligent.

50. For a person to know why they should do something, means for them to understand the benevolent intent of the particular task or activity. It is not possible for a person to act unconditionally in the pursuit of a task that is fundamentally about taking.

Essentially there are two ways to phrase the purpose of a task: on one hand it can be seen to be about the pursuit of self-interest. On the other hand it can be seen to be concerned with making a contribution to the world. We call this second kind of vision, or purpose, a benevolent intent. If you really want to appeal to the best in me as a citizen, to enable me to rise out of my self-serving egocentricity, then give me a vision that makes being a citizen something noble. As South Africans we had something noble in the idea of the Rainbow Nation. This idea was an icon of a society in harmony. As we observed before, it was that intent that was at the base of the success of the 2010 Soccer World Cup.

There is, however, another possibility that we can enact. This other possibility finds its root in the notion that, as South Africans, we are somehow superior to other people. Within the country this chauvinism is what fuels anything from the ongoing racial tension to xenophobic attacks. When this vision of being South African goes abroad we are seen as Africa's new colonists - the MTN in Nigeria, Vodacom in Namibia. It's no surprise that South Africans are not particularly welcome elsewhere on the continent.

The issue of benevolent intent helps to decode colonised peoples' response to colonial occupation generally. It is remarkable that there is so little left of the Dutch in Indonesia, despite the fact that Indonesia had been a Dutch colony from the 17th century. The Dutch left nothing. There is very little trace of them at all. At least the French left their language and baguettes. In India the British left institutions that still survive to this day as does their language, both in Pakistan and India.

So, if we talk about the issue of accountability itself, the argument is thus:

51. It is not just to treat the person who behaves deliberately malevolently, and the person who does so through carelessness, in the same way. A person who behaves malevolently through carelessness should be censured. A person who behaves with deliberate malevolence should be punished. There is a difference between culpable homicide and murder.

If I kill somebody deliberately, this is a different order of harm than if I kill somebody by mistake.

52. The register of correction in the liberal language of justice suggests that inability, carelessness and malevolence are somehow the same thing. This assumption is both false and disastrous. It is unjust to punish a person who is unaware that he is transgressing. It is appropriate to censure a person who transgresses through carelessness. It is appropriate to punish a person who transgresses deliberately. Not to view the person who is malevolent as worthy of punishment is to sanction malevolence in the society.

I would like to give an example by referring to an event that happened at our Zawia[5] in December 2009. A friend got out of the shower one morning and leaned on the basin, which suddenly collapsed. They fell on top of it, got lacerated and ended up having to undergo surgery. The reason for the basin falling out of the wall was that a pipe was leaking inside the wall, to the point that the wall was no longer structurally sound and it was unable to carry the weight of the basin.

I have no doubt that, if this had happened in America or the UK, I would have been sued into selling my children. From a common sense point of view, however, what becomes apparent regarding the issue of accountability if we examine this drama?

Let us assume that none of us were aware of the leak, or we knew about the leak but did not act on it because we did not fully understand the implication in terms of the structural soundness of the wall. The appropriate thing to have done in this instance would have been to use this as an opportunity to learn about the effect of poor plumbing on masonry. There is no culpability here at all, it is just something that you correct.

If we were aware, however, of the potential danger, but we were just ambivalent toward it, then it did not teach us anything, because we knew it was dangerous. It would be perfectly legitimate to punish me and the caretaker of the Zawia. This punishment would still not be as severe as it would be if it was found that we deliberately loosened the bolts in the wall because we knew this man was going to lean on it and do himself an injury.

When dealing with accountability, the key value that operates is fairness. There is a difference in range between the ignorant, the careless and the malevolent. These three possibilities are fundamentally different refractions of the same issue of intent. It is not fair to hold me accountable for what I do not have control over: which is why it would be unjust to punish me if what sat behind the accident was ignorance. If it is determined that I was careless, then I should be censured; but if it is determined that I was deliberately malevolent, then I should be punished.

If the accident is viewed from the point of view of preventing the same thing happening in the future, then my intent would be irrelevant. If I only say I have to correct the problem, I'm treating all three as the same. This is precisely what happens in the register of correction that sits behind the current liberal view of accountability.

This register of correction is very pronounced when dealing with issues related to discipline in organisations. If we saw the caretaker of the Zawia as an employee, the Human Resources function would be quick to caution us not to punish the person, but to correct the problem. If I were absolute about this, then this emphasis on correction disables the possibility of terminal discipline, like dismissal. You cannot correct what you have terminated.

My discipline would, therefore, be biased toward treating the problem as a result of the first variable, a lack of knowledge. It would downplay my intent completely. Viewing my behaviour through the lens of inability, something that I need to be taught, is deeply demeaning. When I am careless or malevolent, it is not because I don't understand something. In other words, when I am careless or malevolent, the just thing to do is execute some sort of retribution befitting to my intent, not just fitting to the infraction.

The emphasis on rights, rather than duties, softens our take on accountability. It confuses accountability with ability issues. They are not the same thing. There are people who do malevolent things not because they have made a mistake, but because they either don't give a damn or are outright malevolent. The man stealing my property is under no misapprehension with regard to whose property it is.

The crisis in governance in South Africa is not because there is a lack of knowledge. There are wonderful institutions teaching wonderful stuff. It's lack of accountability. People aren't ignorant. One of our friends teaches nursing at university. She related an instance recently of a lecturer exchanging exam papers for a duvet cover. This isn't because the person is ignorant, the person is downright malevolent, and this person has a degree! People are intelligent enough to know what the consequences are of what they are doing.

53. If technocratic society requires the brazen pursuit of selfinterest to function, it also suggests that it will harbour a relatively large number of criminally disposed citizens. In fact, a degree of criminality in the population makes a functional contribution to the overall maintenance of the status quo. It cultivates the climate of insecurity, which legitimises the security apparatus of the state.

We need the police because of all the criminals on the street. The police entrench the view that we cannot govern ourselves, that we need to be protected. By handing over our accountability to look after the world around us to the policeman, we are metaphorically settling for the cucumbers of Egypt.

54. The assumption that imprisonment rehabilitates the criminal is both false and arrogant. Prisons foster and cultivate a culture of criminality, they do not remedy it. To imprison the criminal means to punish the victim of the crime twice: firstly, by having been the target of the crime and secondly, by being taxed to keep the criminal in prison. To hold the criminal appropriately accountable for his malevolence means to execute those guilty of violent crimes. Further, it follows that flogging and amputation for less serious crimes would be more just than imprisonment.

While this approach to justice is extreme and can justifiably be accused of being medieval, it has to be seen in the light of the view that dealing with criminality within the context of a generally liberal world view does not seem to work. If South Africa is taken as a case in point, then it is apparent that the sensitive souls who penned our constitution did not consider the following:

• The register of 'correction' in the South African approach to penal matters is clearly misplaced. Very few people are 'corrected' by going to a South African prison. More often than not they come out more criminal than they were when they went in. It is not without reason that jail is colloquially referred to as 'the college of knowledge'.

• There is clearly very little deterrent value in the current approach to crime and punishment. If this was not the case then we would not have the burgeoning prison population that we have at the moment.

• South Africans seem to want a retributive element in legal punishment. If this was not the case, then the popular agitation for the re-introduction of the death penalty would have gone away long ago. It certainly does seem unjust to punish the citizen who is the victim of violent crime twice: Firstly, by being the victim and secondly, by being taxed to house his assailant in prison.

• Looking around the world, it certainly seems to suggest that countries that have a retributive and corporal element to punishment have less crime.

Rights

Paying attention to one's rights in a situation means emphasising what the other owes the self. The focus on rights is therefore similar to the focus on expectation and needs, it cultivates the psychology of a victim in the self and breeds a world view of entitlement. By contrast the focus on duties, places a person's attention on what they should be giving, and therefore cultivates the psychology of freedom. To construct one's intention on expectations, needs and rights is to become the slave and the victim of the other. To pay attention to one's contribution, values and duties is to cultivate freedom. Freedom is concerned with basing one's intention and attention on one's duties, on what one should contribute.

55. The liberal understanding of human rights fundamentally undermines the individual's accountability and, therefore, entrenches his disablement. This establishes the conditions where people are permitted to pursue and remain equal to the worst in themselves. This destroys the individual and the social order at the same time.

Both views that see the intent of the individual as here to take or here to give have elements of narrowness and elements of broadness. They both tolerate and they both judge. What they tolerate and judge, however, are mirror opposites. When the self is seen to be here to get something, there is a tolerance of licentiousness. Any intolerance of licentiousness will only be expressed if the behaviour brazenly affects the wellbeing of others. Because the licentiousness of the individual is accepted as a given, the fundamental approach to keeping order is that it is imposed from outside. Hence the 'nanny state.'

When the view of appropriate intent is that we are here to give, then it is acceptable that we cannot do as we like, even if it does not affect those immediately around us. We are accountable for our own actions. We are, however, allowed to act, to own weapons, defend ourselves in the street, etc. We are not wrapped in legislative cotton wool. We are accountable.

Some time in 2007, I remember seeing a BBC newscast lamenting the flogging by Islamic law of a woman in Nigeria for promiscuous behaviour, and the staggering AIDS statistics of Africa in the same bulletin. Whether it is legitimate to flog someone for adultery is beside the point. What this account demonstrates is the cultural chauvinism of the current western liberal view. This view also judges, it does not tolerate. What is not tolerated is someone being flogged for licentious behaviour. The implications of that licentiousness, however, an unmanageable epidemic of fatal, sexually-transmitted disease, is accepted as a sad fact.

56. The perpetuation of the current order requires the licentiousness of the individual. It, therefore, follows that the suppression of fundamentally destructive phenomena such as promiscuity, pornography, gambling and prostitution will be construed to be contrary to basic human rights.

57. A disabled parent will not be trusted to spank her child. A disabled teacher will not be permitted to exercise corporal punishment on the pupil. A disabled employer will not be permitted to dismiss an employee.

A disabled citizen will not be allowed to defend himself when attacked by a criminal. All of this suggests that the individual is not allowed to hold someone else accountable for their actions. The individual is not accountable, nor can they call someone else to account without the intercession of a super-ordinate control function. The system rules. It is super-ordinate to the individual.

This suggests that the meaning of the worldview that articulates human rights, is hidden in its opposite. Under the guise of promoting the freedom of the individual, the licentiousness that it advocates actually necessitates the imposition of state sponsored control. The more licentiousness that is tolerated, the more control is required. The view of the individual, therefore, becomes one of being increasingly bound and disabled.

If one views the fundamental intent of people to be the pursuit of their self-interest, any expression of perversity will be seen to be a manifestation of a dysfunction buried in the way things are. It will be seen to be an expression rather than a rule. The key issue would, therefore, be not to hold the perverted accountable, but to impose some sort of control, so that this will never happen again.

Organisations

Our examination of how the thematic relates to organisations should be seen in the context of our examination of how surpluses are made. We argued that surpluses are the most immediate measure of the success of an enterprise, and that they only happen when a group of people co-operate in such a way as to produce something bigger than the aggregate of what each individual took out of the enterprise. Organisations, therefore, succeed based on the degree to which the average individual in the organisation gives more than they take.

The initial research work that my colleagues and I conducted under the auspices of the Chamber of Mines of South Africa, as well as our consulting experience since 1990, suggests that there is very little that one can do to an organisation to solicit the intent of the individual to give unconditionally. In our experience, organisational interventions that are concerned with engaging commitment are, more often than not, seen to be cosmetic and seem to entrench the cynicism of employees. Unfortunately,

people generally do not go the extra mile for organisations; they go the
extra mile for people.

To put it another way, we started off trying to understand the
conditions under which people would work for an organisation because
they really wanted to. We discovered that this was the wrong question to
ask. The question is not - 'What is the organisation that people work for
because they really want to?' it is – 'Who is the boss that they work for
because they really want to?'

**58. A company is a virtual village. The requirements for the legitimacy
of the social order are, therefore, equally applicable to the company. A
company that has the enrichment of the shareholder as its primary goal is
basically concerned with the aggrandizement of those in control. It is
therefore malevolent and disabling.**

In the course of the consulting work that we do the most frequent
complaint that we hear from managers is that their employees are not
committed to the business: that their relationship with the enterprise is
purely expedient and that any sense of sincere care is out of the question.
What is even more disturbing is that most of these managers seem to be of
the view that this state of affairs is normative and that it is naïve to expect
anything more. Yet, if you ask the same managers what would account for
their loyalty and willingness at work, they would point out that this
willingness is, firstly, not a function of the organisation but of the
leadership provided by their super- ordinates and, more importantly, their
immediate boss.

If you asked these managers who they would be willing to work for,
they would raise a number of things, all of which could be collated into
two major categories. The first category has a soft and kind ring to it, and
we have come to refer to this category as 'care'. Examples of this category
would be things like: expecting the boss to be empathetic, approachable
and supportive; and to listen. What is interesting about this category is that
people want this care to be unconditional. They are basically saying that
they will not be fully loyal and committed to a boss, who is only interested
in what he can get out of them. They want a boss who has a sincere interest
in them as people.

The second category these managers raise has a much harder feel to it,
because in many of them the consequences for the subordinate are not

necessarily pleasant. It includes things such as fairness, consistency, honesty, being allowed to get on with things and so on. In all of these cases there is a sense of wanting to be accountable for one's own behaviour. If you ask them why they want this accountability, they would argue that this is when one learns or grows. In short, what these managers say, is that they will be loyal to a boss who cares for them and grows them. Not a boss who pays at the top of the range for the industry, or a boss that offers life time security, but a boss who cares for and grows them.

Astonishingly, if you ask employees the same question, they will tell you the same thing. They also want their bosses to care for them and grow them. It turns out that the worker has exactly the same expectation that the manager has, and that is that those in charge should care for them and give them the opportunity to grow. I have found these criteria to be absolutely universal. They are held by people from all walks of life, in the most diverse organisations, from all over the world. I would like to offer an explanation for this phenomenon.

When I work for someone willingly, because I really want to, it implies that when that person asks me to do something, I will probably do it quite happily and willingly. I have given that person the right to demand delivery from me. This suggests that I have given this person the right to exercise power over me, to tell me what to do.

This suggests that care and growth are the criteria which account for legitimacy of power. This makes sense when we examine our first relationship of power, namely the relationship between the parent and the child. In this relationship there are two people, a big one and a little one. The job of the big one for the little one is quite specific. The big person has to care for and grow the little one. Now, in so far as the parenting relationship is the first relationship of power, its significance is that it is a principled relationship. From it we learn what the basic principles of legitimacy are. The principle involved can be articulated as follows:

Any relationship of power is legitimate if the aim of that relationship is the care and growth of the subordinate.

It is, therefore, not at all surprising that most people will invoke these criteria when they consider their commitment to powerful others. It sits within their deepest intuition.

The tragedy is that while managers have these expectations of their bosses, they themselves do not consider it necessary to act consistently with these criteria themselves. This fundamental incapacity of managers to 'do as they would be done by' places accountability for the malaise of carelessness and expediency, which characterises the relationship between employer and employee, squarely at the door of those who are in charge, at every level of the hierarchy. In the most absolute sense, managers deserve the workforce that they have.

Finally, it is important to understand that the essence of growth is about accountability. We previously indicated the usefulness of the metaphor of teaching someone to fish to understand empowerment. If we wanted to empower someone to fish rather than giving them a fish, it is immediately apparent that there are at least two things at issue. One is to give the person the means to do what is required, which in this case would include things such as the rod, the reel, authority to fish and so on. Then, you have to foster the ability to fish, in terms of skill and knowledge. One could refer to these two categories as giving someone the means and the ability to do the task.

These two categories of means and ability, however, are not sufficient to account for the person's fishing, because they do not adequately engage their will. Assume, for example, that you give a person all the means and ability which they require to fish, but then you tell them that they need not be too concerned, because you have a big freezer with fish and if they don't catch any fish you will help them out. Under these conditions they will still not be entirely committed to the fishing enterprise. This indicates that the commitment is only finally accounted for if you hold the person accountable for what they have been entrusted with. Empowerment or growth therefore means to give people the means, the ability and the accountability to do what is required of them. Not to do all three of these things is to disable people.

59. The view that sees organisational structure and system as super-ordinate to the individual is fundamentally Pharaonic. The bureaucratic concern with control both assumes and entrenches the untrustworthiness of the employee at work and the citizen in society. Far from empowering the individual the technocratic order diminishes him at every turn.

A reasonably standard definition of leadership from a business school perspective would be the following from Elliott Jaques:

Leadership is that process in which one person sets the purpose or direction for one or more other persons, and gets them to move along together with him or her and with each other in that direction with competence and full commitment.[6]

Distilled to an essence, the statement is really saying 'Leadership is about achieving a result through people'. This way of looking at leadership in organisations is very common. When we ask leaders in enterprises to define the word 'leadership', we would get a definition consistent with this view in the overwhelming majority of cases. This approach views the achievement of results as the purpose, or the end, of the endeavour, and the people as the means.

While this approach is very common, it contradicts the requirement of Care and Growth at the level of intent. Examine the following two scenarios: Assume Patti has two subordinates, one called Joe and the other called Fred; and assume that Patti is very knowledgeable in a task that both Joe and Fred need to do, because she did that job in 1995; and let us assume that she did it very well.

In Joe's case, Patti walks up to Joe and says: 'Joe, in 1995 I did what you have to do now and what I did worked. Don't argue with me, Joe, do what I did'. In Fred's case Patti says: 'Fred, in 1995 I did what you have to do now and what I did worked. It may be helpful to you to take a look at it.' If the question was which one of these two engagements is consistent with Patti intending to care for and grow a subordinate, it would be the Fred case.

The next question we would want to explore is, what makes these interactions different? It appears as if difference is behavioural. In the Joe case, Patti's approach seems to be autocratic and compulsive whereas in the Fred case, she seems to be more democratic and persuasive. This becomes apparent when one considers who is making the decision. In the Joe case Patti is making the decision, whereas in the Fred case, Fred is making the decision.

At the level of intent, however, there is more going on than is apparent initially. If one separated 'means' and 'ends' in each interaction and put the person, or the result, in either category, the following becomes apparent:

When Patti tells Joe, her end is clearly getting the job done, and by implication Joe is her means or her resource to do so.

Alternatively, if we assume that Patti is being sincere when she tells Fred, then it is apparent that we could have a completely different outcome from what we had in 1995. In fact, it is entirely conceivable that the outcome could be a complete disaster. This implies that Patti's principle aim in the interaction is not to get the job done, it is to teach Fred something. Her end is to enable Fred and her means is the job that he is doing at the time.

Person	Means	Ends	Intent
Joe	Person	Task	Take
Fred	Task	Person	Give
	Person?	Task?	

This distinction suggests a further question, which is, 'Who are the beneficiaries of the two interactions?' Joe clearly experiences Patti as the beneficiary. He, therefore, sees that she is trying to get something out of him. Fred sees himself as the beneficiary. He sees that Patti is trying to give him something. The difference between the two interactions is, therefore, concerned with how the subordinate reads the boss' intent, whether the intent is to give or to take.

If one defined leadership as 'achieving a result through people', then, by definition, one would end up with the Joe interaction. It is in the Joe interaction where the person is seen to be the means and the task is the end. This suggests that, from the point of view of intent, the current view of leadership is deeply flawed. It is the view of Pharaoh, who uses people as his means, to achieve his ends.

The view of Moses, however, makes the task the means and the enablement of the person the end. The question is whether one can run an enterprise successfully by applying this approach to leadership. Our argument is that not only is it possible, but it is the only way to achieve sustainable success. This becomes apparent when one considers the relationship of the coach to a team in the context of a team sport.

Imagine a coach of a team announcing to the team at their first meeting that his job, or purpose, is to get the game played, and to produce the result, and that he was going to use the players as his means to achieve that end. This coach would quickly be in very hot water, with rather disgruntled players looking for a different team.

The reason for this would be that, by doing this, the coach has completely missed the point of what his role is. He is not there to produce a result; the players are there to do that. His role is to coach the player. This does not imply, however, that the coach considers the game that is being played, or the result that is being achieved, as irrelevant. Both of these variables are very important to him, but they are the means that he employs to coach the players. He goes to the game and looks at what is going on the scoreboard, not because these things are his job, but because they are the means for him to do his job, which is to coach the players.

This means to say that the coach, quite literally, uses the task, or the result, as his means to enable the player. His delivery in coaching the player is a change in the competency of the player, and he uses the game and the result to that end. Strangely, when the coach gets this right he is given license by the players to be as tough and as autocratic as he needs to be.

The best coaches are rarely pleasant and affable people. More often than not they are very tough task masters

The question to ask here is, however, 'Who is the beneficiary of this toughness, the coach or the player?' Clearly, it is the player. The key variable that is at issue, as far as the coach is concerned, is not how autocratic or democratic his behaviour is. It is whether his intent is to get something out of the player or to give the player something. This again suggests that the primary variable at the root of leading people successfully, sits at the level of intent. Organisations succeed because the individual goes the extra mile: they give more than they take. This intent to give is solicited by a boss who is there to give to them. Such a boss sees the care and growth of subordinates as his purpose; and the task that is being done, as his means.

Leadership in enterprises cannot be exempt from the rule that requires power to serve those who are submitted to it. Irrespective of the scale of the enterprise, if those in charge of the enterprise do not see that their principle role to is to provide the care and growth of the people working in the enterprise, then what is happening is fundamentally unjust and unsustainable.

Control

Being 'here to give', means an emphasis on process over outcome, whereas, being 'here to get', emphasises outcome over process. Emphasising outcome over process implies a consistent desire to control outcomes. The emphasis on control is manifest at every level of collective life, from organisations, to society as a whole.

60. The more a society is concerned with control, the more it cultivates criminality. The more sophisticated the control mechanisms are, the more ingenious the rogues become.

In a corporate environment, the following example, while hypothetical, would not be unusual. Assume that managers up to a certain level in the organisation have company credit cards that may be used for company business. It is discovered that a manager abused his card for personal gain, and as a result the credit cards are withdrawn from all managers. At the same time, however, it would not be entirely unusual for very little to happen to the manager who abused his card. The bias is, therefore, to control the outcome, rather than to hold the individual who committed the infraction accountable. This may even be seen to be laudable. This is consistent with the view that when things go wrong, one should not have a witch hunt; one should make sure it does not happen again. Far from being appropriate, this kind of response is unjust. It amounts to punishing the many for the sins of the few. Further, because this response does not deal with the accountability of the fellow who abused his card, he remains in the organisation and now has the challenge of finding more ingenious ways to bypass the system.

There is a similar process at work at a broader societal level which is manifested in burgeoning legislation that increasingly restricts the freedom of the individual. Should a small minority of parents brutalise their children, then legislation is passed to ban spanking. This implies continuously writing rules to deal with exceptions.

The effect of the ongoing imposition of control on corporate life is truly debilitating. Because it is the nature of things to go wrong, it means every exception provides an opportunity to impose yet another control. It means that there is an ongoing introduction of control steps in the business process that needs to be managed by someone. Not only does this increase the overall cost of doing business, it also makes the enterprise increasingly inefficient.

61. Each time a control is introduced, one shifts accountability for the thing that is being controlled from the person who is doing it to the person who is controlling it. The effect of this is that the more control you impose, the less power you have.

The following account in 'Leadership: The Care and Growth Model' [7] demonstrates the case. In 1995 I did some work at the Free Gold time office. Free Gold was a massive mine in the Free State, which, at that stage, employed around 80,000 people. The wages for this monster mine were processed at the time office and because of the volume of work, it was a substantial business in its own right, employing around 100 people.

The actual flow of work at the time office was as follows: If a miner did some overtime, the appropriate form would be completed by his superiors and sent to the time office. A clerk in the time office would then take the form, place it next to a data capture form and studiously transfer the information, item for item. The clerk would then staple the two forms together and send them to the supervisor. The supervisor would then separate the two forms and check the data capture form against the overtime sheet to make sure that everything had been entered correctly. If it was correct, the supervisor would sign both forms, send the original to the time office for filing and send the data capture form to the data processing department where a third clerk would enter the information on the system. The net result was that the miner who did the overtime would get the correct amount deposited into his bank account...in theory.

When you are dealing with 80,000 people, there will eventually be a mistake. When that happened, the miner (the overseer) would come to the complaints desk at the time office, armed with his wife, because he drinks far too much brandy and coke, to deal with the problem. His wife, twice as frightening as her husband, calls the clerk who made the mistake over to the complaints desk, howls at them, threatens to beat them up and to shoot her husband if he dares to go underground without the issue being resolved. The clerk's only defence is to turn to their supervisor saying, 'But didn't you check?'

In other words, the supervisor becomes responsible for the quality of the clerk's work because they checked it. If you introduce a checker into the system, you remove accountability for the thing that is being checked, from the person who is doing it, to the checker. You have less control. The more control you impose, the less control you have.

Economy

We argued previously that groups become robust, based on the degree to which the individual gives more than he takes in pursuit of the groups objectives. We also indicated that there was a paradox in this, since the intent to give matures the highest aspects of the self. This maturity culminates in the preparedness for death. This suggests that what we are being prepared for is outside and beyond the social good. Our lives are not subordinate to the social good, the social good galvanises the highest parts of our lives. Although the individual is there to serve the group, the group is there to enable the best in the individual. The best in the individual develops based on the degree to which the individual deals with the other in any given situation with the intent to set the other up to succeed.

In so far as an economy is a subset of a society, the economy is likewise constituted of a set of transactions between individuals. Each one of these transactions either builds or destroys value on the basis of the intent of the individual transactor. The intent to serve, builds value; the intent to get something for nothing, destroys it. Our problem should not be to produce a system that will control the destructive effects of the individual pursuing rampant self-interest. Our problem should be to cultivate the consciousness to serve in those who are transacting.

62. Just as it is illegitimate to ascribe significance to the social order over the individual, it is inadmissible to see the economy as super-ordinate to the transaction. A successful economic order is not one that is well managed by economic technocrats, but one in which each transaction is value adding.

In the same way that society cannot be viewed as super-ordinate to the individual, it is inadmissible to see an economic system as super- ordinate to the transaction. The relationship between the economy and the transaction is like the relationship between the society and the individual. You cannot have a healthy economy if every transaction is unsound. The point of economy is to produce healthy transactions.

63. The language of economics ascribes a scientific validity to a principally speculative exercise. Economic jargon replaces the concern with what accounts for a just transaction with a concern with what kind of system works. It is about what is pragmatic rather than what is right. It trades correctness for expediency.

We should account for the health and illness of the economy on the level of the transaction, not on the level of the economy. The nature of the problem of the transaction is that it is moral problem. It is understanding the difference between a just and a usurious transaction. Any usurious transaction is someone trying to get something for nothing.

When one examines the economy from the level of the whole system, we overlook the justness of the individual transaction. Our principle concern is, therefore, not about what is just. It is about what works. So you shift a moral problem, which is legitimate transaction, to a pragmatic problem – what is going to work. This is a shift from correctness to expediency. This whole economic way of looking at things gives people licence to deal with the problem of transaction with the spectacles of expediency, rather than with the spectacles of justice.

64. A legitimate transaction will reflect the intention of the seller to give good measure and the intention of the buyer to reward service appropriately. The concern for both of these parties is, therefore, what is fair and just for the other, rather than getting as much as possible for giving as little as possible.

The spirit of the transaction is carried by what happens in the negotiation, in the haggle. The current approach to negotiation is fundamentally, about people attempting to get as much as possible for giving as little as possible. The question is whether this is the only possible intent of a negotiation. Surely it must be possible to negotiate in order to establish a just price? It is entirely feasible to have a negotiation with somebody, not in order to beat them, but in order to establish what is fair.

A usurious transaction comes from the intent to get as much as possible for conceding as little as possible. Value adding transaction is based on the intent to give fair value. From the point of view of the self, fair value is concerned with what is clinically fair, plus an increment. As far as the seller is concerned, it translates into the baker's dozen principle. You always have to put in something extra. From the point of view of the buyer, it amounts to paying a premium above the minimum. The sum total of 'that little bit more' is the real wealth of a society. When every transaction in a society is concerned with brazen self-interest, you have an impoverished economy. You have the wholesale rape of resources and the implosion of the system.

65. Any transaction in which someone gets something for nothing is fundamentally usurious and unjust.

66. The degree to which the individual transactions in the market are unjust is the degree to which the market will require super-ordinate control.

When the individual parts are sick, you have to control it from above. If you have illegitimate transaction, you need to have super- ordinate control. You need to control the system, otherwise it implodes very quickly.

67. When the average adult makes doing the right thing their central concern there is little need for overall management of the system. There is a spontaneous order that arises in every sphere of life, from the market to the school. Such a society, basically, works. When the average adult makes getting as much as possible for as little as possible their central concern the social order requires to be managed. Without continuous, super-ordinate control such a society collapses.

68. The modern economy is a hybrid of two tyrannies: an uncontrolled market and illegitimate transaction. This has enabled piracy on a scale unknown in human history.

Stalin could never have achieved within weeks what George Soros achieved with the South East Asian economy. Amazingly, Soros got it right without firing a shot. Modern transaction makes it possible for you to fleece vast numbers of people and never be seen. It enables the surreptitious abuse of people without them even knowing it, because it puts the ghostly fingers of the banking managers of the system, into the pocket of every citizen.

The bankruptcy of the system is evident in the fact that the bankers are not seen to be criminally accountable for the global misery that has followed from the sub-prime debacle. Despite the ongoing dispute about the size of banker's bonuses, they have been seen to have managed the system poorly, and acted in a criminal and morally indefensible way.

COMMENTARIES:

1: See the chapter "The Six Aspirations", in 'Intent' by Etsko Schuitema, Intent Publishing, 2011

2: The Economist, 18th December, 2010 (The Rich, the Poor and Bulgaria - pp 36) quotes a number of studies of happiness in different countries that suggest: 'Latin Americans are cheerful, the ex Soviet Union spectacularly miserable, and the saddest place in the world, relative to its income per person, is Bulgaria.'

3: An Nguni word that can loosely be translated as 'Humanness'. (Nguni languages are a family of Bantu languages that include Zulu, Xhosa and Seswati.)

4: This observation alone should serve to remind us of the futility of the pursuit of corporate careers.

5: A Meditation Centre, Zawia literally meaning 'a corner'.

6: From Elliot Jaques and Stephen D. Clement: "Executive Leadership"

7: 'Leadership: The Care and Growth Model' by Etsko Schuitema, Intent Publishing, 2011

CONCLUSION

The purpose of this text is principally to demonstrate that the issue of intent can serve as golden thread to bind the various disciplines concerned with the human being: from the level of the individual, to the level of the collective. In the course of this I have, therefore, looked at themes that would affect psychology, sociology, economics, the sociology of small groups, business science, social anthropology, and political science. I do understand the arrogance of this endeavour. But I hope that that the reader can overlook my presumption long enough to allow for some reflection on the text as a whole, based on the following key arguments:

1. The fundamental dilemma which the individual faces is the inevitability of death. When the purpose of life is constructed on the basis of accumulation, the inevitability of death renders life futile. When the purpose of life is to give, then death vindicates the dying. Death tests the capacity of the individual to give unconditionally.

2. The process of our maturation is concerned with the process of the maturation of intent to give unconditionally.

3. When I construct my life on the basis of what I want from the other, I become insecure and discontented. When I construct my life on the basis of my contribution, I become secure and fulfilled.

4. When I construct my life on my expectation, I am weak and in conflict with the other. When I construct my life on my contribution, I am powerful and in harmony with the other.

5. Any group succeeds, based on the degree to which the individual in the group contributes unconditionally, in pursuit of the group's objectives.

6. This unconditional contribution is expressed transaction by transaction.

7. When the average adult in the group, irrespective of size, is fundamentally self-interested, groups only avoid implosion on the basis of super-ordinate control.

8. Self-interest produces, and is produced, by control.

9. Power is only legitimate if the intent of the powerful is to care for and grow those in their power.

10. Legitimate leadership is there for those being lead. Illegitimate leadership is there for the leader. Illegitimate leadership uses the subordinate as the means to pursue a task, which has the aggrandizement of the leader as its end. Legitimate leadership uses the task as the means to enable the subordinate.

The significance of all of this suggests that the principle variable that accounts for change, is the individual. All social change, no matter how profound, starts with someone, somewhere. The one is defined by the many, when the one wants to get something. The one defines the many based on what the one is willing to give or forego. You and I, as individuals, are the one. You are the one who can provide the point where the spirit of the age turns from the current, suicidal pursuit of self-interest, to a renaissance of the human spirit.

ABOUT THE AUTHOR

Etsko Schuitema is the founder of the Schuitema Group, a consultancy dedicated to the enhancement of human excellence based on the Care & Growth™ model.

Born into a mining family in South Africa, Etsko grew up in Johannesburg. After doing an Honours degree in Social Anthropology at the University of the Witwatersrand, he got a job as a graduate researcher with The Chamber of Mines of South Africa's Research Organisation.

Employed specifically by the Human Resources Laboratory of the organisation, his work initially focused on the issue of conflict on gold mines in South Africa. At the end of the overthrow of the apartheid regime, the mines were swept up in the upheaval that followed. The work he did led to the development of a framework for understanding trust in this very volatile environment.

Using this basis of this research he was asked to head the Human Resources Laboratory's Industry Project and implement his insights. This is where Care & Growth™ model originated. It was met with significant success within the mining sector. Such success in fact that Etsko left his role with the Chamber of Mines and along with a group of colleagues, to establish a consultancy where this model could be more widely disseminated.

Over the past 30 years, The Schuitema Group under the leadership of Etsko has, alongside several associates, worked in over 26 countries in a large range of sectors, creating powerful working relationships to implement the Care & Growth™ model empowering individuals on all levels of these organisations.

OTHER BOOKS BY THIS AUTHOR